Praise for Peter Rollins's Previous Works

"What Pete does in this book is take you to the edge of a cliff where you can see how high you are and how far you would fall if you lost your footing. And just when most writers would kindly pull you back from the edge, he pushes you off, and you find yourself without any solid footing, disoriented, and in a bit of a panic . . . until you realize that your fall is in fact, a form of flying. And it's thrilling."

—Rob Bell, author of *Love Wins* and *Velvet Elvis*

"While others labor to save the Church as they know it, Peter Rollins takes an ax to the roots of the tree. Those who have enjoyed its shade will want to stop him, but his strokes are so clean and true that his motive soon becomes clear: this man trusts the way of death and resurrection so much that he has become fearless of religion."

—Barbara Brown Taylor, author of *Leaving Church* and *An Altar in the World*

"Rollins writes and thinks like a new Bonhoeffer, crucifying the trappings of religion in order to lay bare a radical, religionless and insurrectional Christianity. A brilliant new voice—an activist, a storyteller and a theologian all in one—and not a moment too soon."

—John D. Caputo, Thomas J. Watson Professor of Religion Emeritus, Syracuse University

THE DIVINE
MAGICIAN

THE DISAPPEARANCE OF RELIGION
AND THE DISCOVERY OF FAITH

PETER ROLLINS

HOWARD BOOKS
A DIVISION OF SIMON & SCHUSTER, INC.

NEW YORK   NASHVILLE   LONDON   TORONTO   SYDNEY   NEW DELHI

Howard Books
A Division of Simon & Schuster, Inc.
1230 Avenue of the Americas
New York, NY 10020

First Howard Books trade paperback edition January 2015

HOWARD and colophon are trademarks of Simon & Schuster, Inc.

For information about special discounts for bulk purchases, please contact Simon & Schuster Special Sales at 1-866-506-1949 or business@simonandschuster.com.

The Simon & Schuster Speakers Bureau can bring authors to your live event. For more information or to book an event contact the Simon & Schuster Speakers Bureau at 1-866-248-3049 or visit our website at www.simonspeakers.com.

Interior design by Kyoko Watanabe

Manufactured in the United States of America

10 9 8 7 6 5 4 3 2 1

Library of Congress Cataloging-in-Publication Data
Rollins, Peter
  The divine magician / Peter Rollins
    pages cm
  1. Christian life. 2. Lord's Supper. 3. Magic—Religious aspects—Christianity. I. Title.
  BV4509.5.R659 2015
  248.4—dc23

                          2014020102

ISBN 978-1-4516-0904-2
ISBN 978-1-4516-0905-9 (ebook)

Eleven,
You are eternal in me.

Contents

Contents

The Sanctuary was empty and the
Holy of Holies untenanted.

—BOOK V OF *THE HISTORIES* BY TACITUS, COMMENTING
ON THE DISCOVERY OF GNAEUS POMPEIUS MAGNUS
UPON ENTERING THE HOLY OF HOLIES IN 63 BCE

INTRODUCTION

❦

Hocus-Pocus

Years ago I was taught how to perform a simple vanishing trick. Taking a quarter from a friend, I'd hold it in both hands and rub it firmly on a tabletop. After this, I'd take the quarter in my right hand, place my left elbow on the surface of a table, lean in close, and rub the coin against my bare forearm. I'd repeat this act of rubbing the coin on the table and then against my forearm four or five times until the coin would finally seem to "dissolve" into my arm. Then, when my friend asked where the coin had gone, I'd lift a nearby pint to reveal how it had been transported magically across the table only to reappear under the glass.

Like most magic tricks, the whole illusion rested on some pretty simple sleight of hand and a little misdirection. The sleight of hand involved getting my audience used to the idea that I always lifted the quarter with my *right* hand after rubbing it on the table. Once this had been established, I would switch and lift it with my *left* hand. With some carefully placed misdirection, people would be momentarily distracted at the point of the switch and so continue to assume that the quarter was in my right hand.

> With some carefully placed misdirection, people would be momentarily distracted.

Manufacturing the disappearance was now a simple matter of rubbing my empty right hand against my elbow, as if the coin were still there, before slowly revealing that it was actually gone.

There was, of course, still the issue of getting rid of the coin that was hidden in my left hand. After all, this would be one of the first places people would look once they realized it wasn't where they expected it to be. This was not, however, difficult to do, for when my left elbow touched the table, my left hand naturally rested at the same level as the back of my neck. While everyone was distracted, I simply hid the coin there.

When the quarter was shown to have disappeared, I'd quickly present both of my hands for observation, thus directing their attention away from where the coin actually was.

In contrast to the disappearance, the return was easy—a few minutes before announcing the trick, I'd clandestinely place a different quarter under a glass on the table. As people were checking my arm and hands, I'd lift the glass to reveal the coin that I'd hidden before the trick even began.

This little illusion contains the three basic elements of a classical vanishing act:

1. An object is presented to the audience
2. This object is made to disappear
3. The object then miraculously reappears

In the film *The Prestige*, directed by Christopher Nolan (adapted from Christopher Priest's book of the same name), these three stages are called:

1. The Pledge
2. The Turn
3. The Prestige

In the coin trick above, we see each of these stages clearly at work. The Pledge represented the part of the illusion where I would ask for a quarter and let everyone examine it. The Turn took place when I made the quarter look as if it had dissolved into my arm. Finally, the Prestige was the point when I lifted my glass to reveal the "return" of the lost quarter.

In addition to these three basic elements—Pledge, Turn, Prestige—a good vanishing act also involves two other components: a little patter (the magician's distracting talk) and the use of some esoteric incantation uttered at the key moment of the Turn.

Both of these elements have some interesting connections with the Christian world.

The term *patter* is most likely derived from *paternoster*, a word that refers to the repetitive, mesmerizing prayers used by nuns and monks in religious orders. For the medieval magician, their own distracting talk had a similar trancelike result as the repetitive prayers of the monks, helping to make the audience less aware of what was going on around them.

In a similar way, one of the most popular "magic phrases" used by magicians in the seventeenth century was *hocus-pocus,* a term most likely parodying the proclamation *hoc est corpus* (this is my body) uttered by priests during Mass.

It was Archbishop of Canterbury John Tillotson who first noted this interesting connection in the late 1600s. In one of his published sermons, Tillotson preached that the magician's words were nothing more than a "ridiculous imitation of the priests of the Church of Rome in their trick of Transubstantiation."[1]

For Tillotson, just as the magician only pretended that something supernatural was happening during the vanishing act, so, too, the Catholic priest deceives his congregants, as he proclaimed that the bread and wine were transformed into the actual body and blood of Christ upon his blessing. Both were stage shows of a sort, a fancy game of deception designed to take in and amaze their respective audiences. Both, Tillotson said, falsely claimed to be part of something supernatural: one in the name of some dark powers, the other in the name of God.

The magician would make an object disappear then reappear.

The priest would preside over the transformation of the bread and wine into the body and blood of Christ.

For Tillotson, *hoc est corpus* was as impotent and ignoble an incantation as hocus-pocus. In pointing this out, he wanted to ridicule and discredit the theory of transubstantiation, exposing it as nothing but a cheap parlor game played by a cynical or naïve institution to confound their congregants.

For Tillotson, the authentic Eucharistic meal had nothing whatsoever to do with superstitious hocus pocus, but was rather a solemn act of ritualistic *remembrance*. Thus, in contrast to the idea of the bread and wine changing their essence, he affirmed the Communion meal's straightforward, pragmatic significance as a *reminder* of Christ's Resurrection in the lives of individual believers.

No doubt the church today would share in Tillotson's desire to distance the Eucharist from a mundane magic trick. Whether they would seek to affirm the meal as an act of remembrance or, instead, claim that something supernatural was taking place, no church authority would equate this central sacrament with that of a mere conjuring act. Any such comparison to playing a game would be wholly rejected.

However, what if one of the best ways of understanding the earth-shattering, deeply life transforming meaning of the Eucharist—indeed, the core proclamation of Christianity itself—is precisely by looking at it *as* a vanishing act?

What if Tillotson was *right* in seeing a connection between a magic trick and the Eucharist . . . but *wrong* in thinking that this took away from its significance and mocked it?

What if we witness this three-part sacramental act as

> What if one of the best ways of understanding the core proclamation of Christianity is precisely by looking at it *as* a vanishing act?

a fundamentally irreligious movement that has nothing to do with theism or atheism, or with doctrines, dogmas, or denominations? But rather as an event that we participate in, an event that takes what we hold as most sacred, makes it disappear before our very eyes, and then returns it to us in an utterly different way.

Through partaking in Communion, the Pledge, the Turn, and the Prestige are sacramentally reenacted. First there is the presentation of the sacred as an object in the bread and wine. Then there is the disappearance of this sacred-object in the consumption. Finally there is the Prestige—the return of the sacred through a realization that we are the body that we consumed, "Now you are the body of Christ, and each one of you is a part of it."[2]

The Eucharist, then, becomes a snapshot of our Christianity as a whole. And looking beyond the Eucharist, I hope to show how Christianity—or rather the "event" that is dimly testified to *in* Christianity—comprises a spectacle that is as scandalous to the world as it is transformative. As we progress, we will see that this event is a stumbling block to the church and foolishness to the cultured elite, but it is good news for the rest of us.

So without further ado, ladies and gentlemen, boys and girls, take your seats and let the curtain rise on what might well be the most incredible, most spectacular vanishing act in the history of the world . . .

SECTION ONE

THE PLEDGE

An Object Is Presented

CHAPTER 1

Conjuring Something from Nothing

The word *Christianity* has largely come to refer to a particular way of viewing the world. It involves a set of beliefs and practices that can be compared and contrasted with other worldviews. Both its advocates and its critics see Christianity as making certain claims about the existence of God, the nature of the universe, and the ultimate meaning of life.

Countless books attempt to work out how the beliefs of Christianity should sit in relation to theories put forth by sociologists, psychologists, and natural scientists. A mammoth amount of time and energy is spent on the question of whether Christianity offers a perspective that complements contemporary theories of the world, conflicts with them, or deals with a different set of issues entirely.

But despite which view one picks, the shared understanding is that Christianity offers a concrete way of understanding the world and our place within it. It is one of the few things that both religious apologists and their adversaries actually agree on—both accept that Christianity makes certain knowledge claims and both accept that these claims attempt to reflect the nature of reality in some way. The only difference is that religious apologists attempt to prove them true, while their adversaries strive to expose them as false.

Whether we accept or reject Christianity, we all seem to know broadly what we mean when we use the term: a worldview that makes certain knowledge claims. Christianity is thus a term that is used to describe a tribal identity; a grouping within society bound together by shared beliefs, traditions, and history.

Of course, within this shared horizon there are legion conflicts regarding what exactly constitutes a Christian belief. Depending on whether one is Orthodox, Catholic, or Protestant (and whether of the conservative or liberal leaning), one will get different answers about which beliefs and practices are debatable and which are nonnegotiable. Some people might only hold a few beliefs as essential, while others might list volumes of things—from the sublime to the utterly ridiculous—that they think we need to affirm in order to warrant the title. All of these different factions, though, agree that Christianity makes at least some claims. Any debates, then, that revolve around what beliefs or practices might be correctly "Christian" continue to operate within the same horizon of meaning.

This belief-oriented understanding of faith causes certain problems for those who find the beliefs unconvincing, who have legitimate doubts, or who suffer from mental health issues that make the forming of such beliefs too difficult. Regarding this last issue, some religious leaders might claim that there is a divine get-out-of-jail-free card for such circumstances, but this very view hints at the idea that belief might not be of central importance.

It suggests that Christianity might concern something deeper than intellectual belief.

Or rather, that something might be happening *within* Christianity that doesn't rest on the affirmation of some church doctrine. Christianity has indeed become another system. It's been reduced to a way of viewing the world and marking out a particular social grouping. However, while Christianity as a system might be of interest to social scientists on one side and systematic theologians on the other, the aim of this book is to chart a different path.

I wish to argue that this founding event—which I will explore as we go along—is not concerned with a set of beliefs concerning the world, but rather calls us to enter into a different way of existing within the world. The good news of Christianity—that is to say the life-giving event harbored within the tradition—is not an invitation to join an exclusive party. Indeed, as I hope to show, this good news involves discovering that those parties aren't all they're cracked up to be, and that there is a way of celebrating life that is more authentic, enriching, and healing than anything we might find through membership to some special club. A way that is not limited to a conservative or liberal, optimistic or pessimistic, theistic or atheistic worldview, but rather one that can operate happily in and through them all.

In order to provide a dim sense of what this event is—or different way of being in the world—I have opted for comparing the good news of Christianity to a magic trick. This is not an arbitrary decision, though there are no doubt other approaches that can be taken. For this reading provides a clear and precise way of understanding how the event of Christianity is not an intellectual position we take with regard to the world, but a way of immersing ourselves in the world.

> The event of Christianity is not an intellectual position we take with regard to the world, but a way of immersing ourselves in that world.

I hope to show that by approaching it through the lens of a great vanishing act, the ubiquitous idea of Christianity as a confessional system of belief, i.e., as involving the affirmation of various doctrines, actually obscures the liberating call that gave birth to this system, a call that encroaches on all religious and secular encampments.

The Creation of the Sacred-Object

In order to understand what this event harbored in Christianity might be, we must begin by outlining a particular type of suffering that we are all prone to. We all face numerous difficulties in life, difficulties that require medical, political, and economic solutions. However, there is one difficulty that would seem to require a different response, one that is expressed and addressed in, among other things, the biblical narrative.

This difficulty can broadly be described as the experience of a *lack* in our lives—a lack we believe can be filled by a particular thing or set of circumstances. For the remainder of this book we shall use the term *sacred-object* to describe whatever it is we think will fill this lack, whether that be money, health, a relationship, or religious practice. Before looking more deeply into the problem faced by this sense of lack, we must spend a little time looking at what makes up this sacred-object, or rather why we would think that some mundane thing would have this magical quality. We can begin by taking a look at the genesis of human beings as described in the Hebrew Scriptures.

The Story of Adam and Eve

In the book of Genesis, we read how Adam and Eve lived in a type of primordial paradise where everything was freely available—everything, that is, except for the fruit of a particular tree: "The Lord God took the man and put him in the Garden of Eden to work it and take care of it. And the Lord God commanded the man, 'You are free to eat from any tree in the garden; but you must not eat from the tree of the knowledge of good and evil, for when you eat of it you will surely die'" (Genesis 2:15–17).

Here, we are immediately confronted with a series of puzzles. For instance, what could possibly make the fruit of this tree so special, and how could it possess the power to bestow moral knowledge? Some readers might be tempted to close the book at this point and dismiss it as mere prescientific nonsense.

However the story is not as esoteric and bizarre as it might initially appear.

In response to the question *What makes this fruit so special?* the answer might be deceptively simple. In my previous book, *The Idolatry of God,* I explored how prohibition can work in relation to a parent and child: if a child is denied a toy, the denial generates an excessive desire in the child for the prohibited object.

The *no* of the parent doesn't extinguish the desire of the child, but acts as a mechanism that *redoubles* the intensity of the original desire. It thus serves to evoke the very thing that it's attempting to quash, transforming an otherwise mundane toy into an object of singular value and importance. What we see in the story of Adam and Eve is the same structure, a prohibition that generates an excessive attachment.

The fruit takes on a special and excessive value because Adam and Eve experience the fruit as barred. Of course objects that are withdrawn in this way don't change in any physical way. But they're off-limits and therefore transformed into a type of sacred-object.

In the example of the prohibited toy, the *no* bestows upon the toy a sacred property that is not an inherent part of the toy, causing the child to find herself deeply attached to it. What was previously only of passing interest now becomes infused with a seductive power. The prohibition can make a mundane object appear sacred, i.e., as something that has the power to satisfy us and render our existence meaningful.

In Robert Duvall's film *The Apostle,* we see a fascinating example of this mechanism at work. In one scene, a racist construction worker drives a large construction vehicle up to a small church with the intention of knocking it down. The pastor of the church, Sonny (played by Robert Duvall), comes out of the church and places a Bible in the direct path of the vehicle. Being raised in the Deep South, the construction worker shows a certain respect for the leather-bound book and gets out to remove it. But Sonny tells him solemnly and with great authority not to touch the book.

> The *no* bestows upon the toy a sacred property that is not an inherent part of the toy.

When he gets closer Sonny asks his parishioners to repeat the words, "No one moves that book."

This prohibition begins to affect the construction worker as he bends down to cast it aside, and at the last minute he finds himself kneeling before the Bible and crying. The prohibition was subjectively inscribed into the construction worker and thus had the effect of transforming the book into a type of magical object before which he crumbled.

Stealing a Masterpiece That Never Existed

Adam and Eve were not forbidden to eat something that would satisfy them, but were faced with a prohibition *that made them think that the fruit would satisfy them.*

In order to understand this, consider the following story.

There was once an artistically talented teenager who felt unrequited love for a girl in his art class.

It so happened that his beloved's artwork was particularly bad, so bad, in fact, that it was often quietly mocked. One day the boy overheard two classmates laughing about how bad her artwork was. But just then she entered the room, and they quickly changed the subject. After a couple of minutes, the two classmates started playing a cruel game where they praised her for her artistic abilities.

She protested, but the classmates kept insisting that she had real talent and should think about exhibiting something in the end-of-year art show.

A week later she pulled the lovelorn boy to one side and asked for some advice about a painting.

He jumped at the chance to talk with her, and while the work was terrible, he praised it profusely. To his horror, the praise he lavished on it convinced her to enter the painting in the school art exhibition.

Because of his love, he didn't want her to be humiliated, so the day before the show he went into the room holding all the submissions and stole her painting along with a couple of others.

Once the theft was discovered, the art teacher quickly worked out who was guilty and pulled the boy out of class. Before suspending him, the teacher asked why he'd stolen the paintings.

"That's easy," replied the boy. "I wanted to win the prize and so stole the best work."

News quickly spread around the school that the girl had created a masterpiece that might have won the prize if allowed to compete.

In this illustrative story, we can see how stealing the bad painting created the illusion that it was a great painting. The removal of a pedestrian thing generated the idea that it was extraordinary.

The subtraction of the painting from the competition effectively added an excessive value to it in the minds of the students, making it into an imagined masterpiece.

The imagined reality was:

- There was a masterpiece.
- It was stolen.
- It could have won a prize.

However the actual reality was:

- A terrible painting was stolen.
- This led to the idea that it was a masterpiece.
- This led to the fantasy that it could have won a prize.

In the beginning the girl may well have thought that she had created a good painting, but the subsequent theft caused her and her classmates to imagine that she had actually created a truly great work. The theft introduced the sense that something wonderful had existed.

With this belief, a new and obstinate sense of dissatisfaction enters the story. The idea that something truly wonderful was taken away initiates a sense of dissatisfaction in the girl. The problem, however, is that the object that promises to get rid of the dissatisfaction doesn't actually exist and so can never be possessed. Hers is not, then, the basic type of dissatisfaction that comes from wanting some mundane thing, but rather an insidious dissatisfaction that comes from wanting a seemingly sublime object that can't actually be grasped.

Both the painting and the fruit exist in a mundane, everyday sense, but the masterpiece is a fiction just as the idea of a super-fruit that would make us gods is a fiction. The seeming inaccessibility of these sacred-objects is what gives them a special halo. But the halo is a lie; the sacred-object is inaccessible and impossible, not simply because access to it is blocked, but more fundamentally because it doesn't exist. The blockage is not what blocks access to the sacred-object, but rather what helps to create the fiction that it actually exists.

> With this belief, a new and obstinate sense of dissatisfaction enters the story.

Virtual Reality

This idea of an object holding an excessive value only in its prohibition or loss forms within us a pleasurable pain (something that is called *jouissance* in philosophy).

It's this very logic that we bear witness to in the story of Adam and Eve. Instead of Adam and Eve first being dissatisfied with the Garden of Eden and imagining that they will be satisfied through transgressing the prohibition (and gaining the fruit), we see that the prohibition is the very thing that creates their sense of dissatisfaction in the first place. When a mundane piece of fruit is experienced as prohibited, it takes on a special value and turns into a sacred-object for the ones who are barred from it. The prohibition thus creates a sense of dissatisfaction. Not an everyday type of dissatisfaction, but a deep sense of gap in the heart of our being that marks every part of our lives.

This ancient story of Adam and Eve, then, offers us a mythical description of how sacred-objects are formed and how their very formation creates within us a sense of painful longing. We (falsely) believe that the sacred-object can offer us wholeness and lasting pleasure; but in actuality, it is responsible for birthing our sense of dissatisfaction. The sacred-object does not exist, yet it cannot be said to simply *not* exist, since our desire for it influences our behavior and drives us to certain actions.

In this way, it is neither actual nor completely fictional.

It is virtual.

In philosophical terms, the virtual is a type of reality that cannot be adequately grasped in the terms *existence* or *nonexistence*. Rather, virtual objects *insist*. For example, fascism doesn't exist in the sense that it would be found in a universe where all people were removed. Yet it still makes its presence felt in society in very real ways.

Whether or not someone is actually a racist, racism can still affect how one behaves. For instance, it might influence where one buys a house, takes a job, or sends one's children to school.

Racist ideology can still regulate people's everyday activities, even if they aren't directly aware of it. In this way, a virtual reality doesn't have to be consciously embraced to be effective.

Grammar also operates as a type of virtual reality in that it regulates how we put words together, yet it doesn't exist in our conscious minds (unless we are studying it). Grammar was there before we arrived on the scene and will be there when we leave. It is something that comes from us and that we are immersed in, yet it is not reducible to us.

This is why one can say that virtual realities *insist*—for they exert force upon us whether we know it or not.

The sacred-object is thus a virtual reality in that it does not actually exist, but makes an impact on us. The sacred-object, as a virtual object, appears actual to us in, and only in, the act of taking it seriously. A virtual reality only begins to dissolve when people *stop acting as if it is real*.

The creation of the sacred-object can be described in the

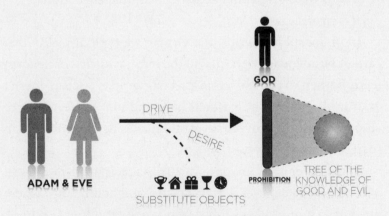

Adam and Eve in the Garden of Eden[1]

following diagram. Here we see how the barrier between Adam and Eve and the tree creates an excessive drive by making the fruit of the tree into something excessively desired. While Adam and Eve can try to content themselves with substitute objects, they remain enchanted by the illusion of what lies out of reach.

I Want What You Want

How we decide which objects are sacred is deeply connected to the desires and interests of the people around us. We find ourselves wanting the things that the people we desire want. If we fall in love with someone, for instance, we find ourselves with desires for a whole range of new things, desires that reflect the interests of the one we are with. If our partner is interested in film, travel, or the piano, we'll often find ourselves taking on these interests for ourselves. In this way we tend to mimic the other's desires and come to experience those desires as our own. This process simply reflects how we constructed desire at an early age within the home.

> We find ourselves wanting the things that the people we desire want.

This means that the things we want, while deeply personal, actually arise and shift in relation to our interactions with others. We can compare this process with something we witness in the 1987 romantic comedy *The Princess Bride*. In one famous scene, a criminal genius called Vizzini (played by Wallace Shawn) gets into a game of wits with the mysterious hero, the Man in Black.

Vizzini fancies himself one of the smartest men in the world and is thus confident when challenged by the hero to a game of wits. The game proposed by the Man in Black is a simple but deadly one in which he places one glass of wine in front of Vizzini and one in front of himself. The Man in Black goes on to explain that Vizzini must choose which glass to drink from and which he wants the Man in Black to consume. However, before the game begins, the Man in Black takes the drinks and hides them from sight for a moment before returning them to the table. He then tells Vizzini that he has added a small amount of iocaine powder, a deadly poison, into the game, one that is both odorless and tasteless.

In response, Vizzini arrogantly states, "All I have to do is divine it from what I know of you. Are you the sort of man who would put the poison into his own goblet or his enemy's? Now, a clever man would put the poison into his own goblet because he would know that only a great fool would reach for what he was given. I am not a great fool, so I can clearly not choose the wine in front of you . . . But you must have known I was not a great fool; you would have counted on it, so I can clearly not choose the wine in front of me."

What ensues is a dizzying monologue as Vizzini works out what he envisions as inspired logic to determine which glass has the poison in it.

Vizzini finally makes his choice, they both drink, and he quickly falls dead.

The scene itself gains its comic effect by enacting an infinite loop in which the criminal gets caught up in a game of "you think that I think that you think . . ." The decision as to which glass to drink is directly connected to what Vizzini thinks is going on in his adversary's mind (the final twist being that the hero actually poisoned both glasses, having previously built up immunity to the poison).

Psychoanalyst Jacques Lacan drew out how our own thinking is connected to what we perceive the other is thinking in an analogy concerning animal tracks. To understand the analogy we can imagine a hunter who is faced with interpreting the meaning of some animal tracks. The initial challenge faced by the hunter is to uncover these tracks and use them as a means of discovering where the animal might be.

However, we can easily imagine a species that masks its true tracks when feeling threatened and makes false ones, so that a less experienced hunter might be misled by the marks on the forest floor. In contrast, the more seasoned tracker will know that the visible tracks are misleading and instead attempt to uncover the true ones.

Yet Lacan notes that there is at least one species we know of that is able to leave true tracks that are intended to be read as false ones: humans.

If I am the one being tracked, I need to judge whether or not the predator is inexperienced. If she is, I might simply run, attempting to gain as much distance as possible from my pursuer, knowing that she likely won't be able to track me. If, however, I know she is more experienced, I might try to cover over my tracks and leave false ones to throw her off the scent. However,

I can also take into consideration what she might think of my experience. Does she think that I'm well versed in survival techniques? If so, then I might decide to leave real tracks hoping that she assumes them to be false and wastes time looking for nonexistent, camouflaged ones.

My reflections could get caught up in a type of infinite loop and must be disrupted by a decisive action if I am to move at all. In the terms of philosopher Jacques Derrida, this would constitute a real decision, for it is a choice that happens when the right move is not obvious. If the right move were obvious, it wouldn't really be a decision at all, because there would only be one true option available.

If I choose to leave true tracks with the hope that my hunter interprets them as false, I am doing the equivalent of telling the truth precisely in order to lie.

Just as our actions are related to other people, so too are our desires. So when asking why a piece of fruit would occupy the space of the sacred-object for Adam and Eve, we can approach an answer by saying that it comes about because each interprets the other as wanting the fruit. The fruit itself isn't a sacred-object because of some inherent property, but rather because of the prohibition combined with an interpretation of what the other desires.

> The story of Adam and Eve is *our* story; it mirrors our contemporary situation.

The Adam and Eve story can thus be read as a reflection of our own situation: we are caught in the gravitational pull of things that we excessively want—

things that are forbidden to us in various ways (by parents, by society, by etiquette, by inability, etc.) and things we think (correctly or incorrectly) others want as well.

The story of Adam and Eve is *our* story; what it describes is not some outdated origin myth, but rather something that mirrors our contemporary situation caught up, as it is, in wanting to find something that removes our lack.

CHAPTER 2

The Curse of the Magician's Curtain

In the previous chapter we explored how the sacred-object is not impossible to grasp simply because something stands in the way of it, but that the prohibition is what calls the sacred-object forth. If we do manage to break through the prohibitive barrier, we discover that what we thought would make us whole actually doesn't.

This means that the very thing we think will make us whole exists only to the extent that we are held back from it. This is the basic message we get from the story of Adam and Eve, as well as from various forms of psychoanalysis. However, it still isn't necessarily clear why the tree that they are forbidden to eat from should be called "the tree of the knowledge of good and evil."

In order to approach an answer to this, we might start by looking at the role of the serpent in the narrative. When we internalize a prohibition so that it generates excessive desire, the excessive desire is often manifested in a type of internal voice.

That voice causes us to question the legitimacy of the barrier by asking whether the "don't" of the prohibition might actually conceal a "do."

When the child, for instance, is confronted with something that is denied to her, a process of rationalization occurs. Rationalization describes the process of creating a set of reasons for justifying what we already desire.

In the Garden of Eden this inner voice is cleverly captured in none other than the serpent, who asks, "Did God really say not to eat the fruit?"

> The prohibition, the sacred-object, and rationalization are all reliant on each other in such a way that getting rid of one means exorcising the others.

This voice speaks to our innermost being and yet is experienced as a foreign body that stands over and above us.

When confronted with a forbidden fruit (the sacred-object), there is always a serpentine presence that torments us. This is one of the powerful aspects of the story—the way that it perceives the fundamental interconnectedness of the prohibition, the sacred-object, and rationalization. They are all reliant on each other in such a way that getting rid of one means exorcising the others.

The prohibition places Adam and Eve in an impossible bind. Do they listen to the voice and transgress the prohibition? Or do they obey the prohibition and content themselves with what is freely available to consume?

The problem here is that neither option is really satisfying; whichever is chosen, regret will follow. In the first option, they break through the prohibition only to find that what lies on the other side is not really some sacred-object but just a mundane piece of fruit. In the second, they content themselves with the fruit within their reach, but always wonder how amazing that forbidden fruit would be if only they could reach out and grasp it.

The Fall

While Adam and Eve might perceive the problem to be how they might get the forbidden fruit, this simply obscures the true problem: how to be free from the excessive drive for the fruit in order to enjoy a life not weighed down by the negative power of the lack that it creates.

The idea of "the Fall," then, is not connected to freedom as some claim. The Fall is not some ideological justification of totalitarianism that warns us about the danger of having choice. The Fall is rather about the oppressive and engulfing power of the sacred-object that enslaves us to an unhealthy obsession. Consider the apostle Paul's antitotalitarian articulation of the Christian collective as a place where *everything is permissible*. This is a claim for radical freedom in which prohibition is dissolved away. For Paul, this place of radical acceptance where everything is permissible, even though not always beneficial, is the great reversal of the catastrophe of the Fall that each of us experiences in our lives.

Paul understood that the prohibition (what he called "the Law") was not the water that extinguished excessive desire, but a fuel that fed it. The problem for Paul was not desire as such, but rather its morphing into an obsessive/excessive impulse through the introduction of a law—a law that tempts us to act immorally precisely by demanding that we act morally.

The Alien Within

So what does this insatiable obsession look like?

To isolate and observe this obsession, we can look at how it is represented in one of the most famous science fiction franchises: *Alien*. At the heart of the Alien films stands the terrifying and unrelenting Xenomorph, a creature that manifests an obsessive drive without restraint. It's a creature that relentlessly and single-mindedly hunts down and attacks humans without fear, fatigue, or reserve.

While the first six films present the alien as a foreign agent that threatens to impregnate and kill the main characters, the seventh film, *Prometheus,* offers an origin story that reveals the alien not as something from outer space, but rather, in the words of Slovenian philosopher Slavoj Žižek, as the symptom of an alien from *inner space*.

In other words, in *Prometheus* we discover that the alien is not some foreign agent outside of ourselves, but rather a foreign agent that is more a part of us than we are to ourselves. In the film we learn that the alien is a material expression of our immaterial drive.

The film itself revolves around a mysterious black substance that has different effects depending on the species it comes into contact with.

Prometheus begins with an explicitly monastic scene in which an Engineer (the name given to the species that created humans) drinks the black fluid and dies. His body immediately begins to break down and falls into the stream of a lifeless planet (presumably Earth). Yet this death creates the building blocks for life to arise on the planet. Later in the film this same substance comes into contact with an android called David. Now the substance remains totally inert. But at the point that humans ingest it, it gives birth to the Xenomorph.

While it has been suggested at various points in the film franchise that the alien is a biological weapon developed by some advanced species, here we glimpse the true origin of the creature:

It is born from a ruthless human obsession.

The black substance gives form to the essence of that which comes into contact with it. It brings into material form the immaterial drive of the species that consumes it.

For the Engineers, who embrace sacrifice and death, the substance brings life.

For the android, which has no inner essence, the liquid does nothing.

Yet when human beings come into contact with it, a type of unrelenting monster is born.

The film's premise is that an old man with almost unlimited wealth is unable to accept his death and has thus funded a deep space expedition in order to find those who brought life to

Earth. In finding these vastly superior creatures he hopes that they might have the key that would prevent him from dying. He's unable to accept his mortality and wants to live forever, but he's not the only one on the expedition who has an obsessive interest in something. The others also are marked by obsessive drives such as the pursuit of wealth, power, and knowledge.

All are seeking something that will satisfy them.

Something that they are willing to travel across the universe to find.

Something that doesn't exist, but that insists.

It's this unrelenting, frenetic pursuit that the black substance births in material form. As author Adrian Bott writes,

> Shaw's comment when the urn chamber is entered—"we've changed the atmosphere in the room"—is deceptively informative. The psychic atmosphere has changed, because humans . . . are present. The slime begins to engender new life, drawing not from a self-sacrificing Engineer but from human hunger for knowledge, for more life, for more everything. Little wonder, then, that it takes serpent-like form. The symbolism of a corrupting serpent, turning men into beasts, is pretty unmistakable.[1]

In *Prometheus* we discover that the Xenomorph is an expression of *us*, something more in us than we realize. We learn that it is a manifestation of our insatiable drive for something that doesn't exist.

It is our pure excessive obsession in material form.

The surprising twist of *Prometheus,* then, is that the alien "out there" is really the alien part of ourselves, that inmost part of us that manifests itself as a foreign agent. Something that is hinted at in the very name of the film, that references the trickster deeply associated with the folly of human striving.

Longevity Without Depth

While death is a reality for all living creatures, in the story of Adam and Eve we witness the description of a death that operates *within* life, a death that is manifested in this incessant inner drive that causes us to act against ourselves. This acts as a major motif in the biblical literature, which often uses the term *death* to describe a form of life rather than the end of life.

For instance, the gospel proclamations that Christ came to bring life—and life, in all its fullness—are not addressed to the literal dead. Likewise, when Jesus is recorded as saying that the dead should bury their own dead, the first reference to the dead is obviously not referring to a biological state, but to those who exist in a state of living death. A living death that can be understood as the suffering both that comes from obsessively desiring something that we think will fill a lack within and that is also manifest in the very com-

> In the story of Adam and Eve we witness the description of a death that operates *within* life, a death that is manifested in this incessant inner drive that causes us to act against ourselves.

pulsion to quell our desire through having such an object. For the desire to rid ourselves of desire is paradoxically a pursuit of death, for it is only in a deathlike state that desire and longing can be extinguished.

What the story of Adam and Eve can help us appreciate, then, is why human beings are caught up in a form of death while alive, seeking something that promises to relieve a type of suffering that it actually causes.

The destructive, obsessive drive that we have been discussing can help us appreciate why unending life could not be synonymous with the theological notion of everlasting life. For if our present lives are infused with a form of death, then the mere continuation of our lives could not be welcomed as a divine gift but rather feared as a demonic curse. If it is true that our lives, even if protected from external traumas, are weighed down by an intrinsic suffering, then merely extending that life would not give it any extra weight or significance. Is this not what we learn from the wisdom of Silenus that Nietzsche so perceptively writes about in *The Birth of Tragedy*?

> There is an old legend that king Midas for a long time hunted the wise *Silenus*, the companion of Dionysus, in the forests, without catching him. When Silenus finally fell into the king's hands, the king asked what was the best thing of all for men, the very finest. The daemon remained silent, motionless and inflexible, until, compelled by the king, he finally broke out into shrill laughter and said these words, "Suffering creature, born for a day, child of accident and toil, why are you forcing me to say what would give you the

greatest pleasure not to hear? The very best thing for you is totally unreachable: not to have been born, not to *exist*, to be *nothing*. The second best thing for you, however, is this—to die soon."[2]

Instead of the mere continuation of life, real good news would proclaim the possibility of a different *quality* of life, one that would have the power to reverse the wisdom of Silenus.

This is what is hinted at in the biblical text itself when we read, "the wages of sin is death, but the gift of God is eternal life" (Romans 6:23). This death of which the verse speaks has no more to do with a biological end than the warning Adam and Eve receive concerning the death that will come from eating the forbidden fruit (after all, they eat it and continue to live). Both speak of a death operating in the midst of life. In contrast, eternal life hints at a type of life that offers a different wage. Not a minimum wage. But a living wage. A wage that renders life truly worth living.

To think of it in spatial terms: this is not about the mere extension of life along a horizontal plane, but about the deepening of life along a vertical plane. Mere longevity cannot render life meaningful any more than brevity has the power to make it meaningless.

A Relationship That Can Never Be

Before grappling with what a living wage might actually look like, we must tarry a little longer with the wage of death, exploring how this obsessive drive for the sacred-object places us onto a fundamentally destructive path.

As we've already explored, the prohibition creates the sacred-object that it seems to hold at bay. In this way, the prohibition also prevents us from directly confronting the fictive nature of the sacred-object. Because this confrontation with the nonexistence of the sacred-object would be traumatic for us, there is a very real sense in which we want to keep the prohibition in place. Why? In order to avoid losing our fantasy that there is something out there that can truly satisfy.

The 1946 film *Brief Encounter* offers us a way of understanding this need for the very thing that we want to break through. The film charts a brief and never consummated affair that takes place between a middle-class housewife, Laura Jesson (Celia Johnson), and a doctor called Alec Harvey (Stanley Holloway).

The story is told from the perspective of Laura, who is sitting at home with her husband, imaging that she is telling him about the brief encounter she had with Alec. It's obvious that her husband is a loving and compassionate man, and it's also clear that she loves him deeply. However, there is something about her emotional and sexual life that remains unfulfilled, something she seems only dimly aware of until she meets Alec while waiting in a train station to go home. She gets some grit in her eye and is helped by the man she will later fall for.

At first she thinks nothing of the help, but they enjoy each other's company and arrange to meet again. While everything initially appears innocent, it soon becomes clear that each has deep feelings for the other. The friendship gradually becomes infused with desire, love, and longing, all of which remain largely unspoken.

In the key turning point of the film, Alec informs Laura that he's staying the night at a friend's apartment close by the train station. He tells her that his friend is out and won't be back until very late. He then invites her to come back to the apartment. At first she declines, knowing that it will lead to some kind of sexual act. All of the obstacles to their relationship are swirling around in her mind: her husband, children, cultural expectations, and friends.

All of which cause her to resist her desire to go back with Alec. Yet, while waiting for her train, she rethinks her decision, decides to act on her passion, and runs to the apartment.

When she arrives the two embrace, but before anything can happen Alec's friend Stephen (Valentine Dyall) suddenly returns. Laura runs from the house and the event becomes the moment in which both come to accept that the relationship is impossible because it would end up destroying too many people. In the aftermath of this failed attempt to consummate their relationship, they agree to part.

What we witnesses at various points in the film is the existence of obstacles that prevent Laura and Alec from touching. Initially these obstacles are presented to us in the usual way: the fact that both are married with children, that their friends would object to the relationship, and that there is a certain guilt about the culturally transgressive nature of their hidden feelings.

But at the very point when their desire breaks through these various subjective barriers and both are ready to meet for an overtly sexual encounter, they are interrupted. Stephen appears at home, almost as if some unseen force had called him back, as if he were a pawn being played by some higher power set on ensuring that Laura and Alec never have sexual union.

Cinematically speaking, the point is not that there is a divine force conspiring against them, but rather that this external barrier between Alec and Laura actually represents an internal barrier operating within Laura. Stephen's appearance at the inopportune moment is the very manifestation of her unconscious fear. He is the final (un)wanted barrier that protects her from gaining her sacred-object. In this way Stephen is in some sense wanted, for without him she would get what she wanted and would finally be confronted with the reality that the fulfillment of her desire is not ultimately fulfilling.

Their inability to consummate the relationship because of some accursed obstacle simply covers the horrifying truth that this consummation is impossible: that sexual union cannot happen. The various obstacles, culminating with Stephen, hid the obvious, though repressed, truth that this affair could never be everything they believe it could be.

In this way they are protected from directly confronting the terrifying insight that the other cannot fulfill them, that there is nothing within their reach that can take away the sense of melancholy that nestles within them.

The objective barrier is then nothing but a concrete cinematic manifestation of a subjective barrier that protects them against a traumatic encounter with the truth: the truth that the sex will not make them one, that any sexual union will ultimately fail to bring union.

What Laura and Alec believe at a conscious level is that the affair could lead to a lasting relationship of bliss and satisfaction; a manifest fantasy that is supported by the very obstacles that keep them from this relationship.

These obstacles do not merely prevent them from gaining what they cannot have; they are responsible for supporting and sustaining the very obstacles they despise. As we learned from the situation with the stolen painting, the obstacle creates what it seems to block. In the same way the various obstacles between Laura and Alec act as the very mechanism that enables the relationship to maintain its electrifying power. It is the obstacle—and climactically, Stephen's arrival—that provides a way for them to ultimately avoid directly facing the suffering involved in their respective lives (an unfulfilling emotional and sexual relationship). They can part company believing that if they had been able to run off together, they might have discovered lasting bliss. Indeed, we, the viewers, are also protected from a direct encounter with the truth. Our own belief in an ultimate satisfaction is left untouched.

> The obstacle creates what it seems to block.

We see this play out regularly in the common cinematic motif of two people with deep feelings almost kissing, but being interrupted at the last moment. It is not simply that the kiss does not happen; there is a sense in which it cannot happen because the kiss is impossible, in the sense of being unable to give what it comes to symbolize within the narrative itself.

It is the very failure to kiss that tempts us to imagine what an amazing future would unfold *if only they could kiss*. In this way the obstacle is often something *we* sustain in order to prevent ourselves from being disillusioned, from coming to know what we already suspect: that the sacred-object is just a fiction after all, and that the other side of the rainbow would be much like the side we're already on.

The Scapegoat Mechanism

This external barrier that prevents us from getting the sacred-object can help us understand the function of a scapegoat. For a scapegoat is that which we blame for not being able to get what we most desire; it is that which takes on the burden of our failure to get what we cannot reach—the sacred-object.

A clear expression of scapegoating occurs when some individual or community is collectively viewed by another to be the obstacle preventing the attainment of their ultimate goal. Something one clearly witnesses in the way the figure of the Jew operates in fascist ideology. In this ideology, the Jew is seen to disrupt the society's organic unity, tribal harmony, and collective identity.

In fascism, the Jewish community takes on the same structural position as Stephen in *Brief Encounter*: as the false problem that prevents a direct confrontation with the real problem. The fascist sees the Jewish community as a problem, when really they act as a type of solution to a problem: *serving to prevent the anti-Semitic community from encountering its own internal crisis.*

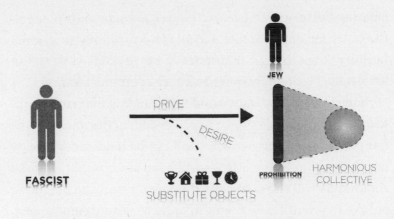

The Fascist's Relation to His Goal

A foreign agent is seen as preventing the attainment of a harmonious and prosperous collective. While the fascist community can attempt to content itself with other things (group meetings, rallies, etc.), its main goal remains unreached, and this means that everything else it does feels ultimately dissatisfying.

However, the foreign agent it blames is actually needed to protect the group from realizing that the idea of a harmonious and prosperous collective is itself a fiction, and that the focused hatred of the Jewish community is actually required in order to maintain a modicum of internal unity and consistency.

Speaking generally, the other is viewed as a type of invader that prevents peace and harmony within a group, yet it is this very belief that allows the group to maintain a minimal level of balance and harmony.

For the fascist, then, the formula for continued existence

involves seeking to remove the Jewish community while simultaneously making sure this pursuit is never wholly successful. In short, it is engaging in a series of horrifyingly violent, but ultimately impotent, gestures that fuel a perpetual war.

If the figure who is fantasized to be holding the fascist community back were ever to be wiped out, then the unconscious fear of the community—that it will not be rendered whole by the obliteration of the other—will be made manifest, and the community will either collapse through schisms and infighting or have to invent a new enemy in order to restore equilibrium.

Historically speaking, we saw this scapegoat mechanism played out in Russia during the early twentieth century when the kulaks were designated class enemies. The kulaks, relatively wealthy independent farmers who emerged from the peasantry, were painted as enemies of the common people. As a result, the state engaged in a systematic and violent persecution of the kulaks—one that involved the seizure of property, murder, imprisonment, and intimidation.

But the more successful this elimination of the kulak was, the more obvious it became that destroying this class was not the answer, but rather acted as a means of eclipsing the real issues. In order to avoid a confrontation with the real problems, the definition of a "kulak" began to expand beyond all recognition. Eventually no one really knew what constituted a kulak. At first they were higher-income farmers with private land, but over time they came to be seen as anyone who hired labor, owned equipment, rented possessions, or was involved in selling or lending on the open market. Indeed it got to a point where local committees were given the right to modify their definition of what a kulak was depending on subjective criteria. Eventually people were being executed for *thinking* like a kulak.

In light of this, Soviet leader Grigory Zinoviev sardonically commented, "We are fond of describing any peasant who has enough to eat as a 'kulak.'"

The unwillingness of the state to confront serious political and cultural problems meant that the kulak was needed to serve as a distraction from real problems.

When confronted with inner conflicts, we are tempted to obscure them by externalizing the antagonisms—something that is done through the hatred of others and/or the hatred of the self (a method in which the scapegoat mechanism is turned inward). The more difficult, courageous, and ethical path involves attempting to face and tarry with the antagonisms. As a prisoner once said to me when commenting upon life as an inmate, "in this place we either face the monstrosity of who we are or we become the monster."

The relationship between the sacred-object and the scapegoat mechanism can help us appreciate why the prohibited tree in the Garden of Eden is associated with morality in the Bible, for it creates situations in which we must attempt to resist being consumed by hatred. This is not a hatred that we see in the animal kingdom, for there we primarily witness a violence that arises from a utilitarian desire to maximize pleasure and minimize pain. In contrast, there is a human violence that goes far beyond this, one that is fueled by an obsession to satisfy an impossible desire to remove a lack that we feel. Something that is hinted at in the anti-Semite who wants to rid the world of the "Jew" and in the lovelorn poet who pines over an unobtainable object of desire.

Not that the pursuit of the sacred-object always plays out negatively for society at large. For that lovelorn poet might end up being a type of Kierkegaard, for much of Kierkegaard's work seems directly inspired by an excessive attachment and repulsion to his beloved Regina. Indeed, many of the great achievements in history could be ascribed to this personally destructive drive. The inability to let go of the sacred-object—whether through directly attempting to attain it or in throwing oneself into an activity in order to try and forget it—can inspire the development of new technologies and great innovations in art.

For the Poor You Will Always Have

In classificatory terms, the scapegoat stands on the outside of a given system. Amid the multitude of different classes (both actual and possible), the scapegoat is the one who is excluded from the class system in its entirety. In this way, the most fundamental conflict is not the one that operates between various recognized groups in society, but rather between these groups and those who are excluded from them. This can be better understood if we reflect for a moment on "Russell's paradox," a name given to the famous thought experiment in which one tries to create a catalogue of "all catalogues that don't list themselves."

The paradox becomes evident if we imagine that the Library of Congress wishes to create a catalogue that lists every library catalogue that doesn't list itself. The problem however concerns whether the catalogue being created should list itself.

If the answer is no, then the catalogue remains incomplete

because it fails to list one catalogue that does not list itself within its own pages. Yet if it does include itself, then the catalogue contains an error, for in listing itself it actually lists one catalogue that does name itself.

Either way the catalogue is a failure.

In an analogous way, this captures how the scapegoat inhabits our world as something that cannot be integrated without rupturing the existing order. The scapegoat is the excluded that unsettles the smooth running of our power structures. Who or what acts as a scapegoat will be different depending on the historical situation (women, Jews, Muslims, the LGBT community), but the excluded "class of no class" continues to exist as the no-things that continually de-center the things that are.

This is why the liberal strategy of opening up communities to previously scapegoated others is not in itself sufficient. In religious terms, some churches are beginning to open up to the idea that gays and lesbians can be equal members of their community. Just as many churches eventually learned to reject explicit racism and sexism, now they are gradually learning to overcome other systems of exclusion. But the problem is that the fundamental structure of scapegoating is not broken in the acceptance of the latest "other." If the underlying scapegoat mechanism is not decommissioned, then new "others" will always arise to protect the

> If the underlying scapegoat mechanism is not decommissioned, then new "others" will always arise to protect the group from its own internal conflicts.

group from its own internal conflicts. For example, people who are gay or lesbian are often being welcomed into the church as long as they seek to embrace the type of relationship configuration endorsed by the church. Instead of being open to different understandings of sexual relationships that might be learned from minority communities who have existed outside the dominant system, these minorities must conform. This is similar to the idea of a church that welcomes someone who is gay as long as he remains celibate. Only now he has a second choice, monogamous marriage for life.

In order to destroy the scapegoat mechanism, a different strategy must be adopted. Instead of trying to create a community where there is no outsider, the real answer lies in understanding that there is a sense in which we are all outsiders. In concrete terms, this means that a community faces its own lack, rather than ignoring it and thus creating a scapegoat who must carry it.

The projection of lack occurs whenever a group seeks solidarity by sharing a hatred of some external group that is directly blamed for a sense of dissatisfaction. Such a group gains its identity from sharing a common enemy. However, it is possible to have a community that owns its lack. One example of this is Alcoholics Anonymous. Here people are encouraged to embrace their alcoholism as a manifestation of their own internal antagonisms. It is this very acceptance of one's own issues that helps provide the atmosphere in which a possible overcoming of the addiction might begin to occur and positive transformation in the alcoholic's relationships can happen.

This is how we can approach the biblical verse that claims

the poor will always be with us. On the surface, it appears to be the antithesis of the belief in a world without poverty. However, we might want to look at it in a different way, acknowledging that a lack is always in existence, and that a barrier to alleviating its worst societal manifestations is to accept its presence in ourselves. Otherwise, we make another carry our poverty in the worst possible way.

The idea here is that the choice is not between a world with poverty and a world without poverty, but between a world where our own internal poverty (our lack) is projected onto real people and one where it is directly faced within ourselves and accepted. So then, the phrase "the poor you will always have with you" can be read as reminding us that we can either tarry with our own poverty or continue to create scapegoats who will become material carriers of the poverty we refuse to face. This doesn't, of course, mean that societal injustice will just dissolve, but rather that effective work can only take place when we address the underlying problems that cause/sustain social evils in the first place.

The move, then, is not between a world of poverty and a world without, but rather between a world where we cannot face our own internal poverty (thus mistreating others and making them poor) and a world where we face up to it and accept it (thus not needing the scapegoat).

In short, the choice is not between a society without outsiders and a society with outsiders, but rather, between a society that sees itself as housing the outside within itself (thus not needing another to represent that outside) and one that refuses to see. It is precisely this idea that fuels Kester Brewin's work of piracy in his book *Mutiny*. There he explores how the original pirates were called "villains of all nations" and who consequently welcomed everyone to join their community. The pirate flag was a symbol of their own symbolic death (death to society), a death that they embraced while still alive. (Interestingly, the skull and crossbones was adapted from a symbol placed in log books beside dead sailors: when someone died, a skull with wings on the side and crossbones would be placed beside the name. The pirates simply removed the wings.)

The point being that the pirates embraced their own status as outsiders and thus were able to set up deeply democratic and equitable communities committed to "a short but merry life."

The Knowledge That We Do Not Know

In light of all the problems that arise from our interrelation with the sacred-object, we can begin to appreciate why the tree in Genesis is called the tree of the knowledge of good and evil. For the sacred-object not only generates an excessive drive, but forces us to take a stand on how we deal with it: either cowardly creating scapegoats or courageously facing ourselves.

> The sacred-object not only generates an excessive drive, but forces us to take a stand on how we deal with it.

This knowledge of good and evil has nothing to do with some intellectual awareness, but with a type of bodily knowing. To understand this, we can simply think about our perception of generic versus brand-name drugs. The placebo effect ensures that more expensive and better-advertised brand-name drugs are more effective than cheaper and relatively unknown drugs, even when both drugs are *exactly* the same. What is more interesting is the fact that giving people this information doesn't appear to make much difference. Even when people know that two differently advertised tablets are the same, a significant amount of people still find that the more expensive brands are more effective.[3] At a conscious level, we may know that the two tablets are the same, yet at a symbolic level the whole industry of advertising has been effective at causing us to experience the two tablets as different. These experiments show how we can know something at the level of the intellect, yet not know it in a bodily sense.

British illusionist Derren Brown has exposed this type of disparity in various interesting ways. For instance, he once hosted a TV show called *How to Convert an Atheist* in which he placed people separately into the crypt of an old church in pitch black for fifteen minutes. All except one started to get scared and began to think that there was some ghostly presence in the room. The interesting thing about the experiment, however, was the fact that none of the participants actually believed in ghosts.

In the same way, whether or not we think we believe there is a sacred-object that will satisfy us and make us whole or that there is an enemy preventing us from grasping it, we can still act as if there is. The virtual reality of the sacred-object may be ridiculed at an intellectual level, but it can still make its presence felt within us at a material level. Indeed, it is even more effective when we don't think about it and merely experience its pull. This can help us render a materialist reading of that old saying that tells us that the greatest trick the devil ever played was convincing the world that he didn't exist. For the sacred-object is a fiction that operates more effectively when we go about our lives thinking it is a fiction.

The Pledge

For Adam and Eve, the sacred-object that caused all their woes was a simple piece of fruit. The fact that this sacred-object in the narrative was such an insignificant thing helps to remind us how mundane and normal our own sacred-objects actually are.

Traditionally the original sacred-object has been depicted as an apple, but for us it might be the desire for wealth, fame, a certain partner, or the birth of a child. There are no limits to how the sacred-object might manifest itself.

The point of the Adam and Eve story is that the sacred-object (whatever it happens to be for us) promises to abolish our sense of lack while actually giving that lack a deadly bite.

The story is a type of mirror that reflects back to us something of our own situation, our own genesis. As I have explored in *The Idolatry of God*, our own entry into the world involves a traumatic experience of lack. And while the objects we imagine will fill that lack change, the idea that *something* can plug it up does not. This original gap occurs the moment we experience ourselves as individuals, for at that moment we feel a

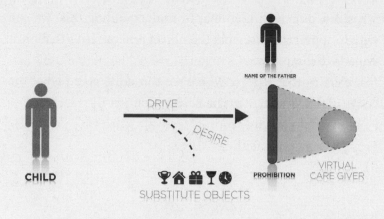

After the Prohibition

separation from our caregiver. This moment is related to what is often called the "name-of-the-father" in psychoanalysis, the name that is given to that which creates/represents the separation.

This separation, while vital for our development, involves a profound sense of loss and a deep desire for that which is believed to have been lost. But just like the fictional masterpiece from the first chapter, this lost object is a fiction. Of course a real caregiver exists; however, there is no way this real person can fill the gap that the infant feels has been ripped away. This marks the formation of the sacred-object in our lives and represents its most primordial form for us. This is our original forbidden fruit.

Like Adam and Eve, the child tries to find satisfaction in other things; however, a connection with this "lost" sacred-object remains.

In the story of Adam and Eve, we find a description of our

own story, our own dilemma. In understanding this, we can begin to appreciate just what the object is in our lives that must be made to disappear.

We are now at a point where we can understand what the Pledge of the Christian magic trick actually is . . .

The sacred-object.

SECTION TWO

THE TURN

An Object Is Made to Disappear

CHAPTER 3

Saint Paul's Optical Illusion

It's only as we come to grips with the constellation of problems connected with the presentation of the sacred-object that we might start to appreciate the real significance of the Turn of the Crucifixion and the Prestige of the Resurrection. A move that takes us from curse to cure or—in more theological terms—from damnation to salvation.

In order to approach a cure, it's important to draw out the connection that exists between Adam and Eve in the garden and Christ on the cross. To do this we will explore the similarity between the conflict depicted in the Garden of Eden and the architecture of the Temple of Jerusalem at the time of Jesus.

The temple itself was composed of three sections:

1. A large outer area called the "Court of the Gentiles," a public place where people offered sacrifices.
2. A smaller area reserved for the priest on duty.

3. The "Holy of Holies," a room concealed behind a huge
   curtain that only the high priest could enter and only
   on the Day of Atonement.

This three-part architectural setup can be seen to closely resemble the physical layout found in the Garden of Eden (as well as the psychological landscape of the child), in that we are presented with two main areas and a barrier that separates them. In the story of Adam and Eve, this barrier is created/enforced by the voice of God (while in childhood development, it is related to the Oedipus complex and described as the "name-of-the-father"). In the temple, the priest fulfills this role.

In the same way that the prohibition created a virtual sacred-object in the minds of Adam and Eve, we can see how the barrier preventing access to the Holy of Holies would create a sense that something amazing lays on the other side.

Those occupying the court of gentiles must content themselves with what lies on their side of the barrier. They buy animals for sacrifice and engage in various trades. However, in the midst of this, they are constantly reminded of their profane position by the curtain that marks a line behind which the sacred is claimed to dwell.

As such we can reproduce the diagrams that express the

> We can see how the barrier preventing access to the Holy of Holies would create a sense that something amazing lays on the other side.

dilemma of Adam and Eve and the dilemma of the child in the following way:

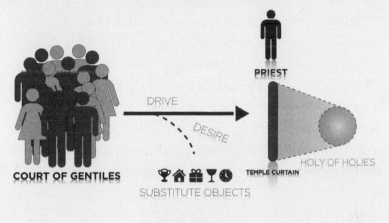

Temple Structure

The idea of the Holy of Holies containing a virtual sacred-object rather than the actual presence of some sacred thing will become clearer in what follows. For now we should simply notice the way that the temple structure mirrors what we find described in the Garden of Eden:

Garden	Temple
Open Garden	Court of Gentiles
Prohibition	Curtain
Forbidden Fruit	"God"

Theologically speaking the temple can thus be read as a symbolic restatement or restaging of the primordial scene of Eden. In short, it provides an architectural representation of the existential predicament described so perceptively at the beginning of the Torah.

The Magician's Stage

In addition to mirroring each other, both the Garden of Eden and the Temple of Jerusalem bear an unmistakable resemblance to the traditional layout of a magician's stage.

The Magician's Stage

The reason for the dotted line behind the magician's curtain is because the object that the magician is going to make "disappear" has already been removed before the "Turn" of the trick. The curtain appears to hide an object, but that is simply an illusion encouraged by the curtain itself and the expectations of those looking on.

In this way we can make the following comparison:

The Garden	The Temple	The Magician's Theater
Open Garden	Court of Gentiles	Front of House
Prohibition	Curtain	Veil
Forbidden Fruit	"God"	Pledge

In order to draw out the connections between what we witness in the temple and a standard magic trick, let us outline the three basic objects involved in a classic vanishing act:

1. an audience
2. the Pledge
3. a curtain

Before the eyes of the audience, the magician places the Pledge behind a curtain, engages in a little misdirection, then rips away the curtain to reveal that the object has vanished.

Typically the misdirection happens when the magician is supposedly placing the object behind the curtain. Just as a child can be fooled by someone who feigns moving a coin from one hand to another, so the magician pretends to set the object in one place while really hiding it elsewhere.

The illusionist thus causes the audience to form a mistaken

belief that the object has disappeared from a place that it never actually inhabited in the first place.

The Magician's Turn from the Perspective of the Audience

The theologically significant feature of such a trick is the way in which the Turn (the point at which the curtain is ripped away to reveal that the object is gone) reflects and reenacts the moment when the temple curtain is torn away to reveal an empty space where God was thought to dwell.

Just as the dramatic pulling back of a curtain by the magician reveals an empty space, so in Christianity the temple curtain was ripped in half to reveal an empty room. In the same way that the audience watching the magic trick falsely believed that the Pledge was behind the magician's curtain, so we believe that the answer to all our problems lies behind the prohibition. The one who experiences the event operating within Christianity is then the one who confronts the falsity of this idea. Not, however, as some kind of intellectual insight but rather through a type of earth-shattering, existential revelation. For this is not about understanding something, but about undergoing a transformation in how we live.

In the same way that participating in a magic trick involves experiencing the shock of being confronted with an empty space where we imagined the Pledge to be, the disciple of the event is shocked to discover that the sacred-object isn't there, that it doesn't exist. This subversive reading of the Crucifixion is one that pulls the carpet out from under the sacred-object established in Genesis. One that reveals that there is no forbidden fruit with the power to make us gods, that there is no sacred-object that will make everything right.

> The subversive reading of the Crucifixion unveils a form of life in which we realize that there is no sacred-object that will make everything right.

The experience of "participating in the Crucifixion" is then the shock of realizing that the sacred does not exist out there in some particular place. This is the *apocalyptic* moment of Christianity that undermines our old way of being. Indeed, the word *apocalypse* refers to both the end of an old aeon and the sudden rending of a curtain. Here the "rabble" that were gathered to witness the Crucifixion are the ones, symbolically speaking, who see the empty room for what it is.

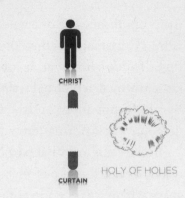

RABBLE   CHRIST   CURTAIN   HOLY OF HOLIES

The Apocalyptic Moment

This revelation places us in the same situation as the Roman general Gnaeus Pompeius Magnus who, in 63 BCE, stepped behind the temple curtain in Jerusalem. According to the historian Tacitus, he was surprised to discover that "the sanctuary was empty and the Holy of Holies untenanted."[1] The experience was not dissimilar to that which is ascribed to the Russian cosmonaut Yuri Alekseyevich Gagarin, who is said to have proclaimed that outer space contained no god.

> This shocking experience of absence lies at the very heart of what it means to experience conversion.

What the claim of Pompeius Magnus and the one reputedly made by Gagarin share in common with the Crucifixion is the insight that the sacred is not to be found in some particular place.

It is this shocking experience of absence that lies at the very heart of what it means to experience conversion—an event that is mostly quashed in the actually existing church, a reactionary space which betrays the scandal of the cross attempting to hold on to the idea of a sacred realm existing somewhere "out there."

Behind the Dark Glass

By approaching the Crucifixion in this way, a radically new and subversive reading of Paul's words in 1 Corinthians 13:12 opens up. Here he writes, "For now we see through a glass, darkly, but then face to face: now I know in part; but then shall I know even as also I am known" (KJV).

In the history of reflections upon this verse, there would appear to be two prime interpretations, both of which view it as an affirmation of some sacred realm lying on the other side of dark glass.

The first is the standard conservative reading in which the verse refers to a time before Christ when we lacked knowledge of the fullness of God. Before Christ appeared, we existed in a type of unknowing with only hints of God that could be gleaned from the nature of the universe and occasional communications via prophets and sacred texts. We dwelled "behind a dark glass," with only an incomplete and partial understanding of the divine. However, in the aftermath of Christ, this indirect and partial revelation is filled out and clarified. This revelation of God in Christ is said to be made available to all via the biblical canon.

In contrast, the standard liberal reading broadly argues that the state of unknowing described by Paul doesn't refer to a time before the incoming of Christ, but rather to our current human condition, limited as we are by our cognitive finitude and particular perspective. As finite, historical, contextual beings, we currently only dimly see the sacred reality that exists beyond the limits of our understanding. Limits that will one day be removed after we have passed from this world.

In the former approach, Christ signals a breaking through of the dark glass that ensures we fully grasp the sacred reality that previously evaded us. In the latter the dark glass has not yet been broken and so we must embrace a certain humility, all the while looking forward to a future time when we will see the sacred face to face.

Despite their surface differences, what both these interpretations hold in common is the underlying idea that beyond our current experience of lack and unknowing *there is a sacred fullness*. So then, while we might currently exist in a state where things manifest themselves as incomplete, this is merely an appearance that results either from the absence of specific revelation (in the fundamentalist/conservative case) or from natural human limitations (in the liberal/progressive case). In this way, both of these interpretations ignore the insight of Gnaeus Pompeius Magnus, opting to read this verse as a defense and justification of the sacred-object. Their only difference lies in whether the partial gaze we have of this sacred fullness is one we all currently suffer under or whether it can be overcome in this life through special revelation.

The assumption here is that whether we know what lies

beyond the dark glass or not, a sacred fullness exists on the other side.

Neither these fundamentalist/conservative or liberal/progressive readings allow for the radical interpretation that we have been outlining thus far: *that the removal of the dark veil doesn't expose a presence on the other side (the sacred-object), but rather exposes us to a traumatic absence.*

While the fundamentalist/conservative reading flies close to this theological airspace (because of the way that they link these verses with the direct significance of the Christ event), it doesn't have the courage to take this reading in a truly irreligious and scandalous direction.

The radical reading of Paul's work on the dark glass is that the event nestled within Christianity signifies the smashing of the barrier, and further, that this destructive act doesn't reveal a fullness, but rather confronts us with the traumatic revelation of an empty space. An empty space that mirrors the Turn of the magician when she removes the curtain to show the audience that the bird is no longer there. The dark glass, then, operates as a type of optical illusion creating the impression that what lies behind it is substantial.

> The event nestled within Christianity signifies the smashing of the barrier and the traumatic revelation of an empty space.

In this reading, it is the "dark glass" itself that falsely gives rise to the illusion that there is something whole and complete on the other side, just as the prohibition functions to create the illusion that there is a sacred-object beyond our reach. The breaking of the dark glass mimics the ripping of the curtain in that it shocks us with the insight that the gap that appears to exist *between* ourselves and the sacred-object is actually the projection of a gap that lies *within* us. More than this, we realize that there is a gap within what we take to be the sacred-object, i.e., that the object we believe will make us whole is itself lacking. In other words, the belief that a gap separates us from what can make us whole and complete hides from us the fact that nothing can do this, for the object we put our faith in is not some Holy Grail. In concrete terms, if we think that another person will fulfill us, we realize that they are as lacking as we are and fundamentally in the same boat. We are then confronted with the idea that we've been duped, deceived into thinking that the gap we feel has some object that can fill it.

It is then a reflection of what we saw taking place in the example of Laura and Alec in *Brief Encounter*, where the various obstacles (culminating with Alec's friend) were actually the things that enabled the couple to defer a confrontation and grapple with their own lack.

If the various obstacles were ever to be removed, Laura and Alec would learn the traumatic but potentially life-transforming truth that what lies on the other side (a relationship) is not qualitatively different from what they already have. The point is not that they should avoid being together, for it may well be better than their current situation, but rather that they shouldn't think it will answer all of their problems. Indeed, one of the things that prevents them from potentially developing a relationship is *the very power of the illusion that it might actually be perfect.*

To understand this, we need only think about the ubiquitous fantasy, propagated across our culture, of a couple who are able to make each other whole, complete, and fulfilled. Not surprisingly, the stories that describe this vision tend to end at the moment when the couple meets, often signaled by the phrase "and they lived happily ever after." What this suggests is that after all the dragons have been fought, the evil stepmothers overcome, and the curses broken, the couple melts into each other's arms and finds satisfaction.

The problem here is not only that such a view is a type of fiction, but that it actually gets in the way of developing what might be a truly enriching, exciting, and enduring relationship. In order to get to a truly enriching relationship, a few stages of disillusionment must first take place.

To begin with, the lover must experience a gap between herself and the object of her love. This can be described as the first manifestation of the traumatic failure. It is the point when she realizes that there are issues that get in the way of her becoming one with her beloved. Whether the two people are in an existing partnership or unable to consummate their love, a crack is revealed that strikes both as horrible. The fantasy is that this gap can be abolished. However, despite those wonderful fleeting moments in which two lovers feel like extensions of each other's being, the gap remains.

Second, the lover must recognize the gap within herself, something that leads to a further suffering. In other words, the gap that separates the lover from her beloved exposes a gap that separates the lover from herself. She feels that the only way she can close her inner gap is to close the gap between herself and her beloved, yet this gap cannot be filled. The first gap is thus redoubled: I cannot be one with myself if I cannot be one with you.

Third, the lover senses a gap within the beloved—that he is not at one with himself. This is also a profoundly difficult insight, not only because it involves the recognition that the beloved is also caught up in the impossibility of ultimate fulfillment, but because it informs her that she cannot be that which makes the beloved whole. She cannot complete her beloved any more than creative work, children, travel, marriage, yoga, or parties can.

Finally, there is the possibility of the two lacks overlapping. Here, the various failures of the previous stages are turned into success. For as the lover learns to embrace the insight that the gap is shared, it can become the very thing that brings both people together. The respective gaps overlap, and both can discover that they are unified in their restlessness, in their ongoing desire, in their frustrations, and in their openness to the future.

The difficulty with the traditional readings of the dark glass is that an extra assumption is slipped in. For it is assumed that Paul means that we will find a sacred fullness on the other side of the barrier, when all that is claimed is that the removal of the glass will give us a clear line of sight to what is on the other side. The truly shocking aspect of the radical reading is that we are confronted clearly with something we already dimly perceive. We already dimly perceived that the sacred-object is powerless to make us whole, but the Christ event fully confronts us with that fact through the act of the Turn.

This contrast between the traditional readings of Paul's reflection on the dark glass and the radical reading is somewhat analogous to the difference we see between Alfred Einstein and Niels Bohr on the subject of quantum mechanics. While Einstein opened up the door to quantum physics, he stayed rooted in a classical conception of the universe. He continued to maintain that the seemingly strange events taking place at a quantum level (such as reverse causation) would one day be able to be reintegrated into the traditional scientific framework.

However, Bohr and his colleagues advocated a more radical vision, namely that the world could not be reduced to some kind of objective, full knowledge, not because of mere human limitations, but because there was an incompleteness built into the very structure of reality itself. They thus saw the newly observed phenomenon as rupturing the traditional scientific framework like new wine might crack an old wineskin. The implications being that the gaps we encounter in the quantum world are not merely epistemological in nature (to do with our lack of knowledge), but rather are *gaps that exist in nature itself*. This new perspective signaled a move toward the idea that what lies on the other side of the observable universe was itself incomplete.

The Gap Within God

In the Crucifixion, we witness this move from the idea that *we* are lacking to the notion that *what we believe will make us whole* is also lacking. For here the narrative describes God experiencing a gap within God (my God, my God, why have you forsaken me). Here the gap *between* humans and the sacred is revealed to be an insight into the nature of the sacred itself—that is, there is a gap *within* the sacred.

This is captured in Paul's phrase, "then shall I know even as also I am known," when speaking of that time when the dark glass will be removed. For to be truly known by someone is also to be known as unknown. For someone to really know us, he must not simply hold positive facts about us, but also grasp the unfathomable abyss of our subjectivity and singularity.

To know someone means embracing the other's inherent resistance to being fully known. To know someone is to know that person as an abyss, as an ever-changing and internally divided subject (which is another way of saying that we acknowledge the unconscious in the other).

This very insight is beautifully hinted at in Christ's cry of forsakenness from the cross, for in his words we witness a theological resituating of the natural gap that we feel *toward* the absolute inscribed *into* the absolute (God experiencing a distance operating within God).

While standard religious systems postulate a kind of separation between ourselves and the sacred-object—whether this is due to our ignorance, misdeeds, or state of being—Christianity draws us into an embrace of the idea that there is a gap operating within the sacred-object itself. Our seeming distance from it is then actually a hint at the very nature of the thing we think we are distant from. In short, the sacred-object does not offer wholeness, because it is not itself whole.

This is a truly novel move because it is all but ubiquitous within spiritual and religious traditions to postulate our separation from some kind of primordial whole. Religions in their traditional and New Age manifestations preach a oneness that we must attempt to regain. But in Christianity, this gap is exposed as existing *within* what we think is whole and complete. At the very heart of the

> In short, the sacred-object does not offer wholeness, because it is not itself whole.

Christ event we see that the gap we experience between ourselves and what we think will make us whole is actually a fiction.

We break through the dark glass.

We walk through the torn curtain.

And we undergo an existential experience in which the incompleteness that we previously thought was due merely to our limits is felt to be constitutive of life itself.

Within the radical tradition this is the scandalous significance of the tearing of the temple curtain and Paul's reflections of it in his thoughts on the breaking of the dark glass. From this lens, we discover that what lies on the other side of the world we know isn't qualitatively better.

This insight is theological in nature, rather than an actual reflection on an empirical fact, for it invites us into a different form of life, one in which we experience the disappearance of the sacred-object and the problems that it creates for us. The insight is thus an *existential* one.

Removing the Curtain

What we are seeing here is the enactment of the second part of the magic trick operating within Christianity; namely its Turn. For while the audience expects to encounter something on the other side of the broken glass, the sacred-object is nowhere to be seen.

The glass is broken.

The curtain torn.

And God—as the garniture of meaning and satisfaction—has vanished.

In this dark revelation we see nothing on the other side and, like Christ on the cross, feel utterly forsaken.

But the truth is that we have really been caught up in an illusion all this time. The sacred-object has not actually disappeared: *it was never behind the curtain in the first place.*

It never existed as an actuality but only insisted as a *virtuality*, as a phantom sustained by the very curtain that appeared to block our access to it.

The magic act operating within Christianity is thus a type of supernatural event in that it is an event that isn't located within nature (as an object of study), but rather changes how we interact with nature.

Understanding that the sacred-object never existed changes how we inhabit our world.

But this affirmation of supernature requires no mystical interpretation. The "supernatural" event does not mean a change that happens within the world, but rather a change of perception that effectuates a change in how we interact with the world.

The supernatural event in which we lose the sacred-object is birthed through the loss of the prohibition, and thus the disappearance of what was prohibited.

We can illustrate how this change in perception occurs through the story of a wealthy judge who went on holiday to Ireland and ended up duck hunting. Halfway through the day, he shot a bird out of the air and it dropped into a farmer's field a few hundred yards away.

As the judge began clambering over the fence, an old farmer drove up on his tractor and saw what had happened.

"What would you be doing there?" asked the farmer.

"I just shot a duck and it fell into this field. I'm going to retrieve it."

> The "supernatural" event is a change of perception that effectuates a change in how we interact with the world.

"Well, now, this here is my property, and that would be trespassing."

"Be careful," shouted the judge, "I'm a powerful man, and I'll make your life hell if you don't let me get that duck."

The farmer considered what he said and then replied, "Apparently, you don't know how we do things in these parts. We settle disagreements like this with the Three Kick Rule."

"What's the Three Kick Rule?" asked the judge.

"Well, first I kick you three times and then you kick me three times, and so on, back and forth until someone gives up."

The judge looked at the farmer and decided that he could easily take the old man on. "Okay," he said, "let's do this."

The farmer slowly got down from the tractor, walked up to the judge, and did a few stretching exercises.

Then he planted his first kick square into the judge's groin, dropping him to the ground.

The second kick was to the side of the head and almost knocked him out.

The judge was flat on his back and in agony, when the farmer's third kick to the abdomen nearly caused him to throw up. But he kept his resolve, knowing that his turn was coming up next.

The judge summoned every bit of strength and managed to get to back his feet. "Okay, now it's my turn," he said.

But the old farmer simply replied, "Naw, I give up. You can have the duck."

We see here how the prohibition creates an obsessive attachment to the duck. The barrier only fuels the judge's initial desire. It is when the prohibition is taken away that he is confronted with the ridiculous nature of his stubborn attachment. What happens here is a mere change in perception instigated by the removal of the barrier.

Crucifixion as Rupture

The Crucifixion marks the experience of losing the obstacle (the prohibition/curtain/dark glass) that sustains our desire for the sacred-object, which we falsely believe lies on the other side.

Because of this, the Crucifixion cannot be reduced to mythology. For a myth is a story that brings meaning, order, and stability to our fragmented experience. It is a narrative that reassures us that everything makes sense, everything has a purpose, and everything is in its place. When confronted by chaos and unknowing, a mythology is a narrative that enables us to cover over the cracks and avoid anxiety.

Creation mythologies, for instance, offer us a way of grasping on to that most perplexing of mysteries (why is there something rather than nothing), reassuring us that the universe is grounded in some higher order. It is perfectly natural for us to construct mythologies in order to make sense of our fragmented and complex world. But by committing to a mythological reading of the Crucifixion, the actual existing church strips away the central scandal of the cross, domesticating the disturbing event that we find there.

Instead, the Crucifixion signals an experience in which all that grounds us and gives us meaning collapses. On the cross Christ is rejected by his friends, betrayed by the religious authorities, and crucified by the political leaders. What we witness then, in the starkest of terms, is the loss of all the structures that ground him and give him the sense that life makes sense (the religious, cultural, and political). More than this, Christ experiences the loss of that which grounds each of these realms by undergoing a death that signaled one was cursed by God.

> The Crucifixion signals an experience in which all that grounds us and gives us meaning collapses.

To enter into the disturbing event signaled by the Crucifixion (the revelation that the sacred-object does not exist) means to experience the limitation of all mythology to ground and give meaning. In this way the Crucifixion experience is nothing less than a type of fundamental rupture that pulls our world off its axis and causes our inner compass to spin out of control. It is the unnerving loss of that which we believe offers stability to our world—whether that be a god, a political party, a philosophical principle, or a way of life.

It is the demise of that which promises us life, but which pays out in wages of death.

CHAPTER 4

The Disappearance
of Nothing

As we've already outlined, the ripping of the temple curtain expresses that aspect of conversion in which we are uncoupled from the oppressive dream of a sacred-object (or, the "Pledge" of the magic trick). Instead of being saved *by* the sacred-object (the promise of religion), the irreligious and subversive event harbored within Christianity expresses a salvation *from* the sacred-object.

In our natural state, we believe that our fundamental problem relates to separation from the thing that will make us whole, yet it is exactly this diagnosis that is the problem. For salvation to mean anything, it must refer to a state of living in which this understanding of the problem is overturned and in which we are freed from what we think we most need.

This freedom means that the salvation we are exploring can't be described as the mere continuation of life into eternity, but is rather of a transformation in the very quality of life, a transformation in which we are freed from the idea that there is something behind the curtain that can make all things good.

Whether or not religion or science can deliver on the promise of unending life, the challenge would remain concerning how to give depth to that life. The case we're building here is that the incendiary event that gave birth to the Christian tradition addresses that challenge.

In contrast to the snake oil claims of religious movements, what we've outlined thus far is the idea that salvation has nothing to do with helping us get what we think will make us whole and complete.

Indeed, it is this very promise that drags us into damnation. The thing we believe will make us whole is the *Pledge* of Christianity, the very thing that Christianity, in its irreligious form, promises to dissolve before our eyes and within our experience.

Salvation—as that which takes place *within* life—means wiping away the sacred-object so that we might find freedom from its gravitational pull.

> Freedom from the sacred-object is not a retreat from life, but a way of stepping into life more deeply.

All of this might make it sound as if the answer lies in simply letting go of desire and making peace with what we have. Yet such a retreat from life and desire is a renunciation that devalues existence by withdrawing from relational, economic, and political concerns. As we shall explore, the freedom from the sacred-object is not a retreat from life, but a way of stepping into life more deeply.

This is not, then, simply a salvation *from* something, but also *into* something. Freedom from the sacred-object simply makes up the second part of the vanishing trick—the *Turn*. There is still a third part to the trick.

If we simply lose the thing we think will make us whole, we can easily find ourselves either withdrawing from life or just moving from one meaningless distraction to another. This second strategy demonstrates an attempt to keep desire alive, but it leaves us open to becoming hollow slaves to the god of consumerism. In order to sustain desire, we become committed consumers of products, ideas, and experiences. We're always looking for something else to keep boredom at bay. The tragic figure of the weary hedonist is the paradigmatic example of this approach to life: he is always partying, but has made hedonism his duty. Every new sexual encounter, friendship, or purchase is just one more experience that can be compared and contrasted with every other. Nothing truly stands out, nothing really inspires, and the world lacks weight.

In contrast, there is an experience of desire that is not oppressive, an experience that offers an alternative to pursuing the sacred-object, retreating from desire altogether, or moving from one ultimately empty thing to another. An experience that is felt most keenly in the experience of love.

When we love a person or a cause, we find something in the world that simultaneously grounds it. The person or thing that we love is *in* our world but also gives meaning and weight *to* our world.

In contrast to something that we treat as the sacred-object, that which we love is not unfulfilling, or rather, the lack of fulfillment found in love is itself fulfilling. What this means is that when we love, our desire is not spent on the object of our love. Our beloved fuels and sustains our desire.

To love is to experience a world come alive, but it also means opening oneself up to a poignant suffering. When we open ourselves up to love, we do not leave pain behind in favor of pleasure; rather we open ourselves up to an experience of depth and meaning that involves both pain and pleasure. For when life is infused with depth and wonder, we cannot help but experience our fair share of both happiness and unhappiness.

It is only in protecting ourselves from love that we can hope to protect ourselves from suffering. By creating a closed circle around ourselves, where we care only for our own well-being, we create barriers that protect us from the storms of life, but that also shield us from life's summer days.

The Forgiveness of Sin

Theologically speaking, we can call this Turn of Christianity "forgiveness of sin." While this phrase has become bogged down with esoteric and obscurantist meanings over the centuries, the argument we are pursuing enables us to give it a very simple and straightforward meaning: the experience of being loosed from the sacred-object.

The term *sin* can be understood as a sense of separation that is expressed in the story of Adam and Eve as the separation they feel from the tree—or the separation religious people feel between themselves and the Holy of Holies. Sin thus relates to all the problems that we have touched on that come from this sense of separation—problems such as the scapegoat mechanism.

Sinful acts, as our attempts to fill that gap, are acts that enslave us to a form of living death. Forgiveness of sin is then the experience of losing this painful sense of lack through the removal of the object we think we are separated from.

The idea of sin thus is not related to a particular act that one commits, whether ethical or unethical, but rather to the way in which a particular act functions in the life of the one doing it. If someone engages in an activity as a means of fleeing the difficulties of life, pursuing wholeness, and extinguishing doubt, then that act can be described, theologically speaking, as *sinful*. In other words, sinful acts are those things we do for the ultimate payoff, a payoff that we never get.

Theologically speaking, that which creates this separation is the Law. So instead of being opposites, *sin* and *law* are intimately connected. Hence Paul famously writes,

What shall we say, then? Is the law sinful? Certainly not! Nevertheless, I would not have known what sin was had it not been for the law. For I would not have known what coveting really was if the law had not said, "You shall not covet." But sin, seizing the opportunity afforded by the commandment, produced in me every kind of coveting. For apart from the law, sin was dead. Once I was alive apart from the law; but when the commandment came, sin sprang to life and I died. I found that the very commandment that was intended to bring life actually brought death. For sin, seizing the opportunity afforded by the commandment, deceived me, and through the commandment put me to death. So then, the law is holy, and the commandment is holy, righteous and good.[1]

Here Paul grasps how the Law and that which the Law attempts to protect us from is actually one and the same thing. He even goes on to say that he was alive "apart from the law" and that the Law brought death with it. In other words, the introduction of the Law brings into the world of life a new form of death previously unknown. Yet Paul is also pointing out here that the Law and sin, while interconnected, are not the same. The Law opens up the vision for a new form of life that it cannot deliver on. This is the problem. For us to get to the new form of life promised by the Law, we must fulfill it in a different way.

> The Law opens up the vision for a new form of life that it cannot deliver on.

In diagrammatic form, we can outline the relationship between sin and the Law in the following way:

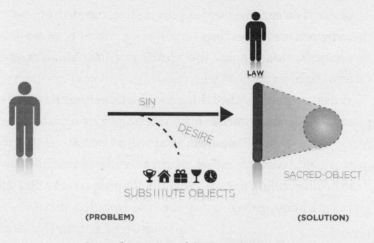

Sin as the Pursuit of the Sacred-Object

What we see here is that the Law creates the illusion of the sacred-object, and that illusion creates a sense of lack. Our attempt to bridge this gap involves various acts that all ultimately fail. These acts are sinful because they are tied up in the frenetic pursuit of an illusion that brings suffering to our lives and causes us to create scapegoats. While we try to make do with various profane substitute objects, none of them offer a fullness of life. We find ourselves caught on the horns of a dilemma, sometimes chasing the wind and at other times distracting ourselves with ultimately unfulfilling objects and experiences.

The Christological Turn then is the realization that the sacred-object that would promise satisfaction is not *found*, but is rather found to be *fictional*.

This realization can be described as forgiveness of sin because *forgiveness* means wiping something out. In contrast to the religious reading of forgiveness as a *payment* of some debt, forgiveness actually refers to a clearing of the slate: *a removal of debt.*

A debt represents something owed, a lack. An IOU note is a piece of paper that stands in for a type of gap, a place where money should be. To forgive a debt does not mean that the debt is paid back, but rather that it is *rendered void.* To pay a debt involves filling the void that the debt represents. But forgiving a debt means saying that the void is voided, that it has no more insistent power, that nothing needs to be paid. Forgiving a debt is the very opposite of paying a debt.

> Forgiving a debt is the very opposite of paying a debt.

If someone forgives a debt, they do not ask for the money, and no one else is required to step in and pay it. Rather, the indebtedness is canceled.

The evidence of "forgiveness of sin" is not found in a profession of belief, but in *a life freed from self-destructive pursuits, scapegoating, and violence.*

The Turn of Christianity thus represents nothing less than the moment of forgiveness, for it signals the loss of the thing we think we need.

In religious terms, the problem humans face is described in terms of our distance from a divine source and the solution involves finding a way (through good works, meditation, Christ, etc.) to bridge the gap. However, the forgiveness of sins, as defined above, places this whole problem/solution matrix into question. Indeed it sees this problem/solution structure *as the problem*. The forgiveness manifested by the symbol of the cross means nothing less than the crossing out of this whole way of experiencing life.

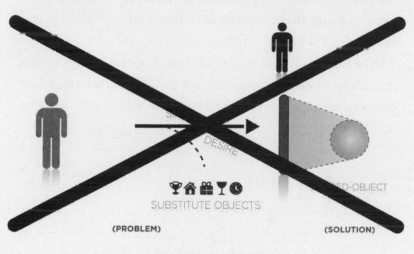

Forgiveness of Sin

This is why the event harbored in Christianity should not be thought of as the means of bridging a gap. This event is nothing less than the smashing of the whole chasm/bridge idea that Gnostic spiritualities buy into. The liberation that this narrative expresses does not offer us the fullness we seek, but rather frees us from the need to seek fullness.

A Way of Being in the World

This way of approaching Christianity as an event involving the disappearance of the sacred-object attempts to draw out in very concrete terms how it expresses a certain way of living in the world—a way that is free from the pursuit of wholeness and satisfaction.

The temple structure is more than an external structure; it captures something of our own internal structure. In theological terms, *we are the temple*. And it is within the temple of being that the temple curtain must be torn down.

THE PRESTIGE

The Object Reappears

CHAPTER 5

Smoke and Mirrors

Until now we have spent time exploring the Pledge and the Turn of Christianity—but a vanishing trick doesn't end with a disappearance. The trick only reaches completion in the Prestige, that moment when we are confronted with a dramatic reappearance.

The Prestige of a magic trick is not, however a mere return of what vanished. It is instead a revealing of something previously unseen that has the *appearance* of what vanished. The bird, rabbit, or coin that the magician brings back is not the original one: it's a substitute.

So what, then, does the Christ event "return" to us? What great apocalyptic return or revealing, which is to say *revelation*, takes place for those caught up in the trick?

The Turn, as we have seen, is the disappearance of the sacred-object that would appear to promise us some escape from this world. It is that experience of uncoupling from the sacred-object's gravitational pull. So if the Prestige of a trick involves a type of return where we get back something similar to that which we lost, yet different, what might that be? We regain the sacred, but not in a fictional thing we can never touch. Rather we receive it back in the form of a depth within things we *can* touch.

In the Prestige, we receive back the sacred, but no longer as an object that seems to dwell just beyond our reach. It returns as a type of ghostly presence that haunts our reality, as an experience of indefinable depth and density in some part of our world.

The Return of the Sacred

The Prestige of Christianity testifies to an experience in which the sacred is no longer that which pulls us away from the profane, but rather is that which emanates from the profane. This is not about some belief in the inherent meaning of things; rather it is living as though *everything* has meaning—a life that cannot help but relate to the world as rich, regardless of what we think. The sacred thus is not some positive thing, but the experience of depth and density operating *in* things.

> The sacred is no longer that which pulls us away from the profane, but rather is that which emanates from the profane.

To grasp the difference between the sacred that we lose in the Turn and the sacred that is returned to us in the Prestige, we can compare and contrast the desire that arises from wanting something we don't have and the desire that is birthed from loving something we do. In the former, our desire is experienced as unsatisfying because it doesn't have what it seeks, while in the latter our desire is fueled by what it does have. In both of these, desire remains; but in the latter this desire is experienced as a positive and life-affirming force.

It does not push us away from the world, but deeper into the world.

We know this desire in the act of love, for in love we don't desire someone we have never encountered, but someone we have. If the love is reciprocated, then the two people experience a desire that enriches their whole world. For when one loves, it is not just the other who takes on value, but the one who loves also experiences a new value in the rest of life.

The desire that is generated by the pursuit of something we believe will make us whole creates a melancholy that creeps into every crevice of our lives, even poisoning our happiness.

This idea of a melancholy hiding within our joy is something that Kierkegaard wrote incisively about in his descriptions of how despair takes hold of us. Under the guise of Johannes de Silentio he once noted that "most people live dejectedly in worldly sorrow *and* joy."[1]

Using the analogy of a dancer, he noted, "One need not look at them when they are up in the air, but only the instant they touch or have touched the ground."[2] For then, he notes, we might witness a small stagger or half-concealed grimace that tells things are not as carefree as we might assume.

It is this pain that dwells in both "worldly sorrow and joy" that is addressed in the divine Prestige. Unlike the melancholy that dwells in both worldly sorrow and joy, it opens up the contrasting possibility of a joy that can exist untouched in the midst of these.

A Failure That Succeeds

This joy does not arise from moving beyond the failure of the sacred-object, but rather in turning that very failure into a success. It means squarely facing the impotence of anything to make us whole and actually celebrating this impotence.

The first step in this journey is one of failure, for in the actual experience of thinking we've grasped the answer we discover that we haven't. This realization cannot but strike us as a type of failure in the very heart of success; for in getting what we want, we discover that it isn't really what we want. Yet it is the very embrace of this failure in the heart of success that can lead to a discovery of success in the midst of the failure.

This move is insightfully brought out by Slavoj Žižek in the book *Less Than Nothing*, when he writes about Hegel's criticism of the crusades.

For Hegel the primary misunderstanding of the crusaders lay in their thinking that the truth of Christianity was connected with the physical place of Christ's tomb.

Yet Žižek notes that Hegel's critique should not be read in the standard way, namely, that the subjective truth of Crucifixion and Resurrection should not be confused with the affirmation of objective claims. Rather, for Hegel, the initial misunderstanding is necessary in the sense that "one has to first occupy the tomb and experience its emptiness," only then, "in this disappointment, through this failure-in-triumph, does one reach the insight that, in order to 'live in Christ,' it is not necessary to travel to faraway lands and occupy empty tombs, since Christ is already here whenever there is love between his followers."[3]

In the journey described here, we begin by fully embracing a religious belief and then experiencing its internal collapse. But this internal collapse serves to create an opening for a deeper insight.

We begin by experiencing the defeat housed in the victory we achieve (getting to the Promised Land), and then experience the victory embedded in the embrace of this very defeat (the Promised Land isn't a place, but is found in every place).

This move is something that we witness in the encounter between Jesus and two disciples who were walking along the road to Emmaus. The moment these two disciples realize that they are with their Messiah, he disappears (failure in the success), yet this very disappearance is accompanied by an internal presence represented through the experience of a burning deep within their hearts (success in the failure).

> We begin by experiencing the defeat housed in the victory we achieve, and then experience the victory embedded in the embrace of this very defeat.

By avoiding a confrontation with our own failure, we will not get to the point of experiencing this deeper victory. It is possible, for instance, for a couple to avoid a confrontation with their own failed marriage as long as certain questions are not asked. Perhaps it's obvious that the husband is being unfaithful or that the wife is no longer in love, but as long as neither person brings up the obvious reality, the relationship continues to function in a minimal way. The point is not that the relationship lacks a crisis, but rather that the crisis is not being acknowledged and thus its effects are not directly confronted.

The effects are still *indirectly* felt, however, perhaps through fits of anger, alcohol abuse, or depression. Here the failure of the relationship is repressed, and so movement to some healthier place is closed off.

It is this type of refusal that we see play out in the well-known parable of a rich businessman who, while returning to work after lunch, saw a fisherman get up from the side of a river with a bucket of fish.

"Where are you going?" asked the businessman.

"To the market to sell these fish," replied the fisherman.

"And how long did it take you to catch those?"

"A couple of hours."

"Well, what are you going to do for the rest of the day?"

"Oh, I don't know," said the fisherman. "I guess I'll just go sit on the beach with my family, drink wine, and chat to passersby."

"But if you keep fishing you could catch enough to earn more money!" said the businessman.

"And why would I do that?"

"Well, you could buy better equipment to catch more fish. Within a few years you'll have enough for a boat and a large net. Why, eventually you might even own a fleet of boats!"

"And then what?"

"Why, then you could sit on the beach with your family, drink wine, and chat to passersby!"

What we are confronted with here is the way that the businessman fails to see that the path to his own ideal *is* a type of failure. His own work has failed to give him the very thing he wants. We see that he could actually have the very thing he seems to want, if only he could acknowledge the failure of his current position.

For Those with Eyes to See

The divine Prestige, here, resembles the insight of traditional atheism in that the sacred is not located in some distant place: *the Holy of Holies is empty.* But this loss holds within it a profound gain, for the resurrection testifies to a Return in which the sacred is revealed as having no place in the world and then, in the blink of an eye, is discovered in the lived experience of care and concern for the world. In the

> The Resurrection testifies to a Return in which the sacred is revealed as having no place in the world and then is discovered in the lived experience of care and concern for the world.

very failure that comes from ripping away the curtain and finding that the temple is empty, a success becomes possible.

This transformation in how we dwell within and interact with the world is not a new belief about the world. Instead, it is a way that one relates to the world regardless of one's beliefs. It is not irrationalism in the sense of being against reason, but neither is it a rational proposition that can be argued for. It is not analogous to blindness nor is it an ability to see something that others can't.

It is rather a *way* of seeing what is already clearly visible.

Of perceiving or receiving what already is given.

This approach is captured in the idea of God as *love*. For God as love expresses the idea that the sacred is not found in a distant object toward which we focus our love, but rather is testified to in the act of loving itself.

Faith, then, is not a set of beliefs about the world. It is rather found in the loving embrace of the world.

Because the actual existing church has reduced the Crucifixion and Resurrection to religious affirmations held by a certain tribe, rather than expressions of a type of life, the event they testify to has been almost completely eclipsed.

The Idol and the Icon

Theologically speaking, one might say that the Turn and the Prestige testified to within Christianity signal the disappearance of the *idol* and the appearance of the *icon*. The idol is simply a theological term for the imaginary thing we believe will make us whole, while the icon is a way of holding something that draws us into an experience of wonder and awe. In contrast to an idol, which eternally stands outside our world, an icon is in our world.

While the idol is always at a distance, the icon is present.

Yet the icon does not abolish distance, it rather relocates it. To treat someone or something as an icon is to experience a type of force field that causes our desire to "revolve," not quite hitting its target, yet remaining close.

When someone is an icon for us, his very presence is experienced as a mystery. Whereas, in the previous diagrams, there was a bar separating a person from his idol, in the diagram below this bar is situated *within* the other. For in the icon, there is still something that resists being known, but this is not because we are separated from it. Rather, the unfathomable mystery lies within the icon itself. The icon is with us and yet there is something about it that is yet to arrive. It is experienced as having a depth and wonder that is not closed down in its presence, but rather opened up and intensified in it.

Relationship to the Icon

In theological terms, the icon's presence can be described as a type of *realized eschatology*, meaning that its presence is experienced simultaneously as a foretelling of something that is still to come. This "to come," however, is not temporal in nature (to be one day consummated), but is part of the very structure of love itself.

The icon thus doesn't satisfy desire, but rather throws desire into a different register—one in which we are not fulfilled, but rather where our desire is emboldened, deepened, and robbed of its melancholic yearning.

The experience of the Crucifixion/Turn is thus the disappearance of the idol so that we might encounter the Resurrection/Prestige in which some part of our world is opened up as iconic.

> The iconic way of being helps us experience the mundane as infused with special significance.

When we are caught up in idolatry, we focus on some special object that makes everything else in the world seem mundane. In contrast, the iconic way of being helps us experience the mundane as infused with special significance. In theological terms, this is the idea of God in the midst of life.

The Body of Christ

Through partaking in the Eucharist, the Turn and the Prestige are sacramentally reenacted. First there is the presentation of the sacred as an object in the bread and wine. Then there is the disappearance of this sacred-object in the consumption. Finally there is the return of the sacred through a realization that we are the body that we consumed, "Now you are the body of Christ, and each one of you is a part of it."[4]

Contrary to the religious reading of the Eucharist endorsed by the actual existing church, this antireligious and subversive reading helps us approach what might be the truly scandalous message contained in the meal. A meal that cuts against the very root of religion, that overturns the church in its actually existing form, and that invites us to experience a new intensity in life.

CHAPTER 6

The Empty Cabinet

In the aftermath of the great Prestige, faith is no longer shackled to the idea of something "up there" in a place that we will one day reach, but describes our loving embrace of this world we inhabit. Far from abolishing a sense of hope, embracing the world can help us appreciate hope's truly risky and subversive nature. Religious conceptions of hope approach it as something safe and secure—as a hope in something that will come to pass and thus doesn't require our active involvement. It is a hope that encourages passivity, a hope that allows us to accept our current conditions in the belief that something better is galloping over the horizon.

But the hope that comes from letting go of the idol is risky. It's a type of hope without hope, a hope against hope. It's a hope that makes demands on us, that calls out to us, and that asks us to put our weight behind it. It is a hope that tells us we can make the world a better place, that we can transform society and enact justice, but only if we put our effort into it. In the words of philosopher Walter Benjamin, it is the hope that we might become the messianic answer to those before us who cried out for justice. While we cannot bring back those who have been tortured, abused, cursed, and killed, we might be able to help forge a world that they had once prayed for. To hope is to heed a call—a call to act.

This type of hope isn't safe. It's not untainted by the contingencies of life. It's a hope that is rooted in the earth and one that we must tend to, feed, and protect if we want to see it bear fruit.

To hope is to plant our efforts in a field of risk. It involves committing ourselves to the idea that better is possible, and opening ourselves up to the very real possibility of disappointment and depression.

We see how this type of hope plays out in our relationships. For example, if we hope that our child will one day go to university, the hope doesn't cause us to sit back and do nothing, but rather to try and make sure that she gets a good primary education. When we love someone as she is, we accept her as she is, yet we work to make her life better, to enrich it in some way that might dimly testify to the way that her existence has enriched us. To have hope for those we love is to give ourselves to their betterment, to be motivated by the idea that their life could be richer.

> To have hope for those we love is to give ourselves to their betterment.

The event testified to within Christianity is evident in a life that has been freed from an idolatrous existence that turns us *from* the world to an iconic engagement *with* the world.

The Critique of Signs and Wisdom

This freedom from the sacred-object also spells freedom from the need to find an overarching meaning to life. Indeed, the apostle Paul directly attacks the idea of Christianity offering a system of meaning in his attacks on what he called "signs" and "wisdom." Signs and wisdom represent two ways in which we seek meaning. Through either apologetic argument or the occurrence of unusual or unexplainable events, we want to find ways to justify our beliefs.

While the affirmation of signs and wisdom to justify a particular religious position is part and parcel of religious discourse, Paul sets his sights firmly against them when critiquing the Jewish community of his day for seeking the former and the Greeks for wanting the latter,

> Jews demand signs and Greeks look for wisdom, but we preach Christ crucified: a stumbling block to Jews and foolishness to Gentiles, but to those whom God has called, both Jews and Greeks, Christ the power of God and the wisdom of God. For the foolishness of God is wiser than human wisdom, and the weakness of God is stronger than human strength.[1]

What's fascinating here is the way Paul sets up the Crucifixion as the very opposite of a sign or wisdom. From the perspective of both, the Crucifixion can strike one as nothing but empty nonsense. Why? Because this method of execution symbolized a divine curse. More than this, the idea of an innocent man, let alone God, being murdered in such horrific terms strikes against the idea of justice, reason, or goodness.

It is a meaningless, absurd, and offensive event, something theologian Paul Hessert picks up in his book *Christ and the End of Meaning,*

> Anyone executed by hanging was seen in Jewish tradition as cursed by God. The sign of such a death was taken as divine corroboration of the administration of human justice. In other words, God was seen as acting in this sign-event to give the victim "what was coming to him."[2]

As that which runs against the very idea of a sign, Hessert argues that what we're confronted with is a type of profound offense to reason:

> The affront is not merely the case of the ignominious, brutal death of Jesus . . . [it is] to the whole religious outlook that searches for signs. . . . Preaching "Christ crucified" is not merely saying that bad things happen to good people but that God's approach to us belies our expectations.[3]

In other words, the event of the Crucifixion is actually the very contradiction of our expectations. This contradiction is much more than the liberal concept that the cross represents the idea of a good person being killed because he stood up against injustice. It is rather a direct confrontation of all that we think religion and God are about—it is that which breaks apart "our sense of reality."[4]

In the scripture passage quoted previously, Paul connects the desire for wisdom with the Greeks and their development of classical philosophy (the "love of wisdom"). The Greeks were not so much interested in signs, but rather with the eternal realm of ideas. They sought an underlying rational structure that would make sense of the passing, decaying nature of the world and render it all meaningful.

The preeminent teachers of wisdom at the time of Jesus were the Stoics. Stoicism was the ancient Hellenistic philosophy that emphasized an emotionally balanced life based upon a will that was in accord to nature, a strong moral temperament, and a deeply rational outlook.

These teachers would often compete with Christian preachers for an audience and argued that behind the chaos of our lived experience there was a harmonious center, an order that could, in principle, provide a meaning for everything. The Stoics saw the brokenness and decay of the world as a type of illusion or temporary condition. While they had a strong moral theory, there was a broad acceptance of the status quo. In this way, Stoicism was able to become the philosophical outlook of the cultural elite in the Roman Empire without actually threatening some of the more barbaric and inequitable practices of the day.

The Stoics would have had little problem in accepting the liberal reading of Christ's crucifixion as an example of one who faced injustice and suffering with peace and resoluteness. Indeed this Jesus would have fitted very neatly into their worldview.

For Paul, however, there was something much more profound and offensive taking place in the idea of "Christ crucified." Indeed, Paul was reading the Crucifixion *against* this stoic vision of Jesus. For Paul, the Crucifixion was that which defied reduction to a sign or system of meaning. As Hessert notes,

> "Christ crucified" makes no sense. Instead of linking God to the enveloping rationality that absorbs or even overrides the passing contradictions of goodness, it focuses attention on the contradiction itself. That is, "Christ crucified" is no key to the meaning of life and human events. It is a *problem* to meaning, a problem requiring explanation.[5]

Hessert notes that the Shoah operates in a similar way within Jewish thought. For the Shoah is that horrific, unspeakable event that ruptures and renders offensive any attempt to make it into a divine sign or element of wider rationality. This is why the term *Shoah* is often preferred over *Holocaust*. For the latter is derived from the Greek *holókauston*, a term that has connections with the notion of religious sacrifice and thus religious significance. In contrast, the *Shoah* simply means destruction and thus lacks any justificatory undertones.

The attempt to provide a cosmic meaning for the Shoah is not simply misplaced, it is a profound offense.

The attempt to provide a cosmic meaning for the Shoah is not simply misplaced, it is a profound offense. The event stands as an affront to all such strategies. In terms of the European intellectual tradition, the First World War can be seen to act in a similar way. One of the features of this horrific event is found in the way that the war disrupted all our attempts to tie it into some deeper meaning or significance.

It is precisely this connection with meaning, religious or otherwise, that the Crucifixion of Christ cuts against.

Once we grasp this idea of Christ representing a break with signs and wisdom, we can begin to perceive how the actual existing church has fundamentally betrayed the scandal of the Crucifixion, effectively making it into a type of Stoic doctrine that doesn't challenge our world, but confirms it.

In contrast, for Paul, "Christ crucified" is that event that defies all attempts at being reduced to some system of meaning.

It is a type of antisign that fractures religious signs.

An antiwisdom that confounds human wisdom.

A nuclear event that blows apart all of our apologetic enclosures.

The Empty Box

This means that radical Christianity is fundamentally antagonistic to all ideological systems, for ideological systems are those frames that provide stable meaning and justification for the status quo. Whether they rely on ideas like fate, history, or progress, ideological systems justify the way the world is against revolutionaries who seek to challenge it.

The sad reality is that Christianity has become the paradigmatic example of an ideological system. Since being wedded to the state with Constantine, the church has been justifiably viewed as serving the interests of those in power by placating those without power. The general view of the enlightened secularist is that the church is neck deep in the ideology of the world it finds itself in—either through direct justification or by telling people not to worry about the current state of the world because things will be better in the next one.

Not only this, but churches are ideological in that they create their own constellation of beliefs and practices that tell their congregants how to think and behave. A denomination, for instance, will offer dogmas, doctrines, and rituals that to a greater or lesser extent let everyone know how to interact with the world.

In this way, the church offers people guidelines concerning both the law and what it means to transgress that law. Even though most people in the church won't know what many of these laws are, they still find themselves subject to them, being rewarded by staying within acceptable practices and punished for stepping outside of them.

Yet ideology is more complex than this, for an ideology not only provides a set of rules describing what is acceptable and what is unacceptable, but also tells us the acceptable ways in which we can go against what is acceptable: *it tells us both how to conform and how to not conform in a conformist way.*

Take the example of a family where sleeping with a partner outside of marriage is viewed as morally unacceptable. Many such families offer a clear sense not only of what is right and wrong, but of the right way to engage with what they judge to be wrong. For instance, a married couple might accept that their daughter has sex with her partner as long as she sleeps in a separate room when visiting and doesn't talk about the fact they live together. If these criteria are met then everything carries on as usual. This logic can be outlined in the following way:

LAW: Don't sleep together.
ACCEPTABLE TRANSGRESSION: You can as long as we all pretend you aren't when we're together.

In more explicitly religious terms, we can see this relationship between the law and acceptable transgression in the way that some churches relate to the question of doubt. In a conservative church, doubt may well be unacceptable (or doubt about certain central doctrines), yet it is often acceptable to have doubts, as long as you don't share them in a formal church setting.

I remember talking with a woman who confided that she had doubts concerning a literal resurrection. She was an elder in her church and a longtime worship leader, but she told me that if she spoke publicly about her doubts, she'd likely be asked to step down from her position. I asked whether she thought the other elders might have similar questions. Her response was telling: "Well, I suppose they must, I mean, many of them have been doing this for years. I really can't imagine that they don't." In other words, if she was correct, the real transgression in her community lay not in having doubts about the Resurrection but in speaking them. We can outline this in the following way:

LAW: Don't doubt the Resurrection.

ACCEPTABLE TRANSGRESSION: You can, just don't talk about it in church.

UNACCEPTABLE TRANSGRESSION: Talk openly about it in church.

Indeed, the church informs one not only how to transgress the laws of the community, but *when* to transgress them. For instance, a church might preach the verse that claims a person of faith can drink deadly poisons without being affected, but people would think you were mad were you actually to act on this (for example, by drinking a household poison to see what it tasted like).

This idea of law and its acceptable transgression is a central insight of Žižek's theory, and is captured well in the analogy of a king and his jester.

The jester, or fool, was a court entertainer who, in addition to performing tricks, was able to joke with and even mock royalty. Indeed, Queen Elizabeth once chided her jester for not being cutting enough in his humor. A jester, however, walked a tightrope, for if he was too mocking, he left himself open to punishment or even execution. Thus he had to transgress the court in a way that was acceptable to the court. In short, his transgression had to be endorsed by the very system it seemed to act against.

This can help us see how the person who transgresses in a way that is acceptable to the system he is part of is not a thorn in the side of that system but is actually an important part of it. Indeed, such fools are needed by the system in order to allow its people a certain edgy pleasure that helps facilitate the smooth running of the machine.

"Backsliding" provides an interesting case in point. If someone considers herself a backslider, she is defining herself both within and against the system that she is a part of. As a backslider, she is accepting the religious position that she is transgressing against. Because she defines herself in relation to it, she continues to support its truth even though she acts against it.

> Such fools are needed by the system in order to allow its people a certain edgy pleasure.

Backsliders thus have a position within the system they fall short of, even though this position is generally a lesser one. More than this, backsliders will often return to the fold in time; either giving up their old ways or learning how to engage them in ever more acceptable forms. Indeed, a "backslider" is often simply one who hasn't yet realized that what he is doing is actually possible within the very heart of the system itself, as long as he manages it well and doesn't talk about it.

In contrast to the jester, the trickster is someone who transgresses against a system he is part of in a way that genuinely jars the system itself. The trickster is a revolutionary figure who is able to expose the reactionary moral, political, and cultural thinking that closes an ideology in upon itself and cracks it open to real self-interrogation and transformation. Tricksters will look very different from each other, depending on their context. For they do not share similar beliefs so much as they share a similar structural position within a particular system of belief. They act, then, as a type of new wine that ruptures old wineskins.

The point here, however, is that the radical collective, which is built upon fidelity to the event housed in the name of Christ, stands fundamentally against both unquestioned submission to ideology and to playing the role of the jester who attacks it in a futile and token way.

The radical Christ collective seeks not only to help people experience the ripping of the temple curtain in their own lives, but to feel the power of a subversive sign that ruptures all signs and a truly transgressive wisdom that confounds all wisdom.

This means that the radical church is dedicated to rupturing our most basic ideological commitments as well as striving to expose how the enlightened secularist is actually knee deep in the ideology he disavows.

The way that the radical Christ collective exposes the cultured despiser to his own ideological commitments is succinctly captured in an old Irish story that tells of a competition that asked people to construct the largest possible sheep enclosure using a limited set of materials. Three people entered: an architect, an engineer, and an old farmer.

On the day of the event, each of them was given some basic tools, a pile of wooden planks, and twenty-four hours to complete their pen.

When it came time for the judges to decide the winner, they began by examining the architect's work. She had used her extensive knowledge of buildings to construct an impressive circular structure that maximized the utility of the materials. Nothing went to waste, and a hundred sheep could easily be held inside.

Next, they looked at the pen created by the engineer. His was more simply constructed but four times the size of the architect's. He had also used all of the material, but he had spent much of his time studying the strength of the wooden planks and worked it out that he could split them without compromising the security of the pen.

Last, they came to the old farmer who, in contrast to the others, was surrounded by unused planks and large bags of nails. They watched in disbelief as the farmer carefully stepped into the two-foot square box he'd made.

"That's your enclosure?" said one of the judges, laughing in disbelief. "Why, you hardly fit inside! How are you expected to get even one sheep in there?"

"Don't be silly," replied the farmer. "I'm on the outside. You're standing in the enclosure!"

Here the judges mocked the farmer, thinking that he was inside the sheep pen, when it was really the farmer who was on the outside. By experiencing a rupture within one's system of meaning, the radical church offers a rupturing of ideology in the sense that it is the space in which ideology (as the system that provides meaning) is questioned and cracked. It's not possible to dwell in such a space for long, for there is no real existence outside of ideological constructions. However, there is a way of briefly being shocked out of one's ideology in a way that means one reenters it in a critical way, becoming more aware of what was previously just assumed. The result is a new type of relation toward one ideological system, an antagonistic relation evidenced in the figure of the trickster.

In contrast to the trickster, it is the figure of the cultured despiser who is most uncritically immersed in ideology today, and it is the role of the radical Christ collective to expose this.

For is it not the case that the secular world is enslaved to all kinds of sacred-objects that promise satisfaction? From relationships to health, wealth, and glamorous lifestyles?

Is it not obvious that the secular world is immersed in signs that show people how to be satisfied (advertisements, movies, commercials, etc.) and wisdom that justifies the pursuit of wholeness (New Age spiritualities, magazine articles, self-help gurus, etc.)?

Is it not true that the secular world has its prosperity preachers, its snake-oil salesmen, and its peddlers of false paradise?

> The claim of the radical collective is that a form of religious ideology is alive and well in the secular world.

The claim of the radical collective is that a form of religious ideology is alive and well in the secular world.

In response to the mocking claims of those who point and laugh at the radical collectives for being the ground zero of ideological justification, there is one answer: "You think that you're outside of ideology? Can you not see? You're standing in it!"

From Belief to Faith

In order to drive home the point that the Crucifixion is not about justifying a religious ideology, Paul employs the word *faith* rather than *belief* or *sight*.

Today the word *faith* is, by and large, employed as a way of expressing the belief that there is some underlying force working for the greater good, intervening to ensure that everything will work out well in the end, regardless of the surface appearance. Like the religious conception of hope, this idea of faith doesn't require our involvement, for whatever happens does so for a *reason*, and the reason is *good*. Even if something terrible happens that a believer doesn't think is good—for example, the murder of a child—the argument will be made that this is the cost for a greater good, such as being an unfortunate result of having moral freedom.

In contrast, there is a different way of understanding faith that operates outside the realm of meaning making. This is a type of faith against faith. A faith that involves us. One that is full of risk and uncertainty.

What is interesting about this faith, however, is that there is still a type of confidence in the midst of the uncertainty—but this confidence operates in a different register.

We can approach the nature of this confidence by reflecting on the unconditional commitment expressed in love.

If we believe that the world is meaningful—yet do not love—we cannot help but experience the world as meaningless. However, if we believe that the world is meaningless—yet we love—we cannot help but experience our world as meaningful. There is in love a type of confidence that expresses itself in utter commitment and confidence. Yet this is not directly connected with any intellectual affirmation. Indeed, the confidence of love is best seen whenever there is a lack of intellectual confidence.

Take the example of a couple, deeply in love, that is considering marriage. If we were able to convince them that the relationship was likely doomed (for instance, showing them divorce statistics), they would likely not care in the least. For to love someone involves not balking at risk or uncertainty, but rather acting regardless. If the couple rethought their position when confronted with evidence of the likely failure of their relationship, we would wonder if perhaps their decision was based on more pragmatic grounds. The confidence that comes from love is not connected with the rational weighing of evidence or the endorsement of a system of belief—to paraphrase Pascal: it is a reason of the heart that reason cannot know. To borrow a term from philosopher Jacques Derrida, faith can be described as *undeconstructable*. What this means is that faith is a type of ethereal call that invites us into a loving and passionate commitment to the world. In response to this call, we create beliefs and systems that attempt to embody this commitment and put it into action.

At best, these systems can be deeply transformative; however, they can never take the place of faith. Faith not only demands that we create systems, but reminds us that any structure we form is ultimately made for people; people are not made for the structure. Faith thus demands that we both form views and opinions about how best to live in the world and acknowledge that these views need to be fluid, open, and rethought in relation to new situations.

This understanding of faith as undeconstructable can be compared to the example of a young man complimenting his fiancée. He might say that she is beautiful, wonderful, smart, thoughtful, gentle, passionate, and funny. But no collection of these adjectives is able to properly encapsulate why he loves her. As long as the love continues to grow, new words will replace old ones and none will capture the love absolutely.

Someone else might see all the same qualities in the woman that he does and yet remain indifferent to her. It is not that the lover sees some additional property that the other fails to grasp, but that he views his beloved in a way that the other doesn't. It is not that he "sees" more than another person, but rather he holds what is seen *differently*.

The woman might have lots of attractive attributes, yet she is not reducible to them in the eyes of her lover. He experiences her as irreducible to any collection of properties. His love for her means that she is experienced as uncontainable and unnameable.

The *motivation to compliment* is the result of a love that cannot be put into words. The lover senses an indefinable core in his beloved that causes him to put forth an unending litany of compliments. The undeconstructable is that which motivates the words, not the words themselves.

In a famous passage from the apostle Paul, we see this distinction in action when we read:

If I speak in the tongues of men or of angels, but do not have love, I am only a resounding gong or a clanging cymbal. If I have the gift of prophecy and can fathom all mysteries and all knowledge, and if I have a faith that can move mountains, but do not have love, I am nothing. If I give all I possess to the poor and give over my body to hardship that I may boast, but do not have love, I gain nothing.

Love is patient, love is kind. It does not envy, it does not boast, it is not proud. It does not dishonor others, it is not self-seeking, it is not easily angered, it keeps no record of wrongs. Love does not delight in evil but rejoices with the truth. It always protects, always trusts, always hopes, always perseveres.

Love never fails. But where there are prophecies, they will cease; where there are tongues, they will be stilled; where there is knowledge, it will pass away. For we know in part and we prophesy in part, but when completeness comes, what is in part disappears. When I was a child, I talked like a child, I thought like a child, I reasoned like a child. When I became a man, I put the ways of childhood behind me. For now we see only a reflection as in a mirror; then we shall see face to face. Now I know in part; then I shall know fully, even as I am fully known.

And now these three remain: faith, hope and love. But the greatest of these is love.[6]

When Paul writes against "hollow and deceptive philosophy, which depends on human tradition and the basic principles of this world,"[7] he is making it clear that the life of faith is not some worldview that can be learned in school. One could have the perfect philosophy and still be nothing but a clanging cymbal.

The person of faith is not known by which philosophical outlook she affirms, but rather by her commitment to life. She can take any stand or no stand concerning the meaning or absurdity of the universe, for faith does not operate at that level. The lived certainty of faith has nothing to do with belief or nonbelief in gods, natural law, or karmic returns. It has no regard for metaphysical systems or carefully constructed worldviews.

> Faith describes a lived protest against forms of life that treat existence as worthless.

It instead describes a lived protest against forms of life that treat existence as worthless.

The Miracle of Faith

The word *supernatural* is almost universally tied to a religious worldview. Regardless of whether we affirm the supernatural or deny it, the term seems inextricably and necessarily connected with belief in higher powers. Interestingly, however, this religious definition of the supernatural is concerned almost only with the purely natural realm. For instance, miracles are ascribed to physical occurrences like a resuscitation of someone who was dead or the feeding of a vast crowd with a few loaves of bread and a handful of fish.

In contrast, there is a different way of approaching the supernatural, one that doesn't see it as describing a change in the natural realm, but rather as describing a change in how we interact with the natural realm (hence supernatural). This is a view of the supernatural that can be affirmed by the theist and the atheist alike.

Here a miracle isn't directly encountered in the resurrection of someone from the dead or in feeding a vast crowd of strangers with crumbs (amazing as these acts would be). Rather it is indirectly glimpsed in that change in our life when we judge a person worthy of being brought back to life, or when we discover a compassion that makes us believe a crowd of total strangers should be fed. The miraculous is then testified to in that moment when we come to feel that life has infinite significance.

Thus the true miracle of faith is not something natural, but something that takes place *in* the natural.

It is something that is analogous to how one might relate to music. In purely physical terms, music is powerless to transform anything. It cannot raise the dead, cure heart disease, or bring back a lost lover. Music does not change the world we live in, reverse time, or transform history. Neither does it promise practical solutions to life's woes.

But music is anything but impotent, for it can assist us in changing the way we interact with the world in which we live.

It can help us to affirm life, embrace it, and sublimate it.

Music can help sensitize us to and celebrate the life that we participate in.

So, too, with poetry. The poet is one who can help us experience life as inscribed with a rich and sensuous texture. She can help us call forth, confront, and confirm our existence, inviting us to find a courage that might enable us to say yes and amen to life in the midst of its complexity and in spite of our anxiety.

In this way we might begin to appreciate how a real miracle is not something that raises the dead, but something that raises the living to a place where life is not experienced as death.

A divine miracle is not something that simply raises the dead, but something that raises the living to a place where life is not experienced as death.

INTERLUDE

Trickster Christ

So far we have outlined the event harbored in Christianity in terms of a three-part illusion containing a Pledge, a Turn, and a Prestige. Before progressing to how we might begin to conceive of collectives in which this magic trick is played out, let's take a moment to see how this entire approach plays out in relation to the gospel telling of Christ.

In order to do this, let us begin by contrasting the project of Christ as found in the Gospels with the famous story of the prodigal son. Before exploring the differences, let us spend a moment reacquainting ourselves with the story:

Jesus continued: "There was a man who had two sons. The younger one said to his father, 'Father, give me my share of the estate.' So he divided his property between them.

"Not long after that, the younger son got together all he had, set off for a distant country and there squandered his wealth in wild living. After he had spent everything, there was a severe famine in that whole country, and he began to be in need. So he went and hired himself out to a citizen of that country, who sent him to his fields to feed pigs. He longed to fill his stomach with the pods that the pigs were eating, but no one gave him anything.

"When he came to his senses, he said, 'How many of my father's hired servants have food to spare, and here I am starving to death! I will set out and go back to my father and say to him: Father, I have sinned against heaven and against you. I am no longer worthy to be called your son; make me like one of your hired servants.' So he got up and went to his father.

"But while he was still a long way off, his father saw him and was filled with compassion for him; he ran to his son, threw his arms around him and kissed him.

"The son said to him, 'Father, I have sinned against heaven and against you. I am no longer worthy to be called your son.'

"But the father said to his servants, 'Quick! Bring the best robe and put it on him. Put a ring on his finger and sandals on his feet. Bring the fattened calf and kill it. Let's have a feast and celebrate. For this son of mine was dead and is alive again; he was lost and is found.' So they began to celebrate.

"Meanwhile, the older son was in the field. When he came near the house, he heard music and dancing. So he called one of the servants and asked him what was going on. 'Your brother has come,' he replied, 'and your father has killed the fattened calf because he has him back safe and sound.'

"The older brother became angry and refused to go in. So his father went out and pleaded with him. But he answered his father, 'Look! All these years I've been slaving for you and never disobeyed your orders. Yet you never gave me even a young goat so I could celebrate with my friends. But when this son of yours who has squandered your property with prostitutes comes home, you kill the fattened calf for him!'

" 'My son,' the father said, 'you are always with me, and everything I have is yours. But we had to celebrate and be glad, because this brother of yours was dead and is alive again; he was lost and is found.' "[1]

This parable has achieved a greater cultural and religious significance than most other stories from the Christian scriptures. Indeed, it has been repeated over generations in the West as one of the primary means of understanding what divine love, acceptance, and forgiveness look like.

However, writer Kester Brewin overturns this reading by offering a provocative alternative in his book *Mutiny*.[2] Instead of seeing this as a story of repentance, love, grace, and forgiveness, Brewin gives us a disturbing rereading that shakes up the religious interpretation. Rather than seeing this as the story of a son's rebellion and a father's magnanimous forgiveness, he asks what might happen if we view it as a tragic tale describing a failed revolution.

This subversive reading begins by explicitly bringing to mind the profound wealth and privilege of the family that stands at the center of the narrative. This is a family that knows neither want nor need. It is a family of three, who are protected from the harsh realities of the world through the ownership of vast land, property, cattle, and, in all likelihood, slaves.

Brewin notes that in this family there is "a grouchy and overly-dutiful older brother who had no choice, as the first-born, but to work in the family business." But there is also a younger son who glimpses an opportunity to escape the shadow of his father and throw himself into an adventurous exploration of the world. The story begins with this younger son addressing his father with a demand for his share of the inheritance.

We don't know the motives for the son's desire to leave. Perhaps he wanted to make his own way in the world. Or maybe he didn't like the conservative way that wealth was viewed by his family and sought to spend his share on creating new experiences, making new friends, and seeing things he had never laid eyes on before. Alternatively he might have seen himself as a humanitarian figure, taking his wealth and using it to help those in need.

Regardless of the motives, the protagonist is soon faced with a world very different from the comfortable one he left. The young man encounters deep poverty and real need. Indeed, a famine devastates the land, and he soon experiences this poverty firsthand. For probably the first time in his life, this young man learns what it is to have an empty stomach—and even ends up taking a job on a farm that pays so little he covets the rotten scraps that he gives to the pigs.

This is the crisis moment of the narrative, for it's the point where the protagonist is faced with a problem that must be overcome. The soon-to-be prodigal is poor, hungry, and working a terrible job, so he devises a plan.

He no doubt knows that he can always return to his father's palatial estate, but he's reluctant. He has a certain discomfort about going back to the old ways of living off the wealth of the family and being under the parental authority of the father. So rather than return as a privileged son—living off the fat of the land—he decides to return as a hired hand.

> Rather than return as a privileged son—living off the fat of the land—he decides to return as a hired hand.

In this way he will be able to do an honest day's work and perhaps get an honest day's pay.

And so the story goes that this young son returns to his father's home, tired and thin, but also resolute. However, things don't quite work out as he imagined. His father, who has not ventured out into the world to look for his son (an interesting departure from other similar parables that speak of a farmer actively seeking his lost sheep and a woman looking for her lost coin), hears that his son is coming back. Delighted at his son's return, the wealthy father runs out to greet him and reintegrate him into the safe haven of the family home. He wants to hear nothing of the son's strange ideas about becoming an honest worker and shuts down the conversation:

> His father refused his pleas to have him work. He gave him a warm robe, which, if a little heavy on his thinned frame, felt sumptuously comfortable. He was given the family signet ring, which invested him with an odd feeling of pride. He was someone again, with a strange but alluring sense of power. This didn't seem to be the time or place to challenge his father and persuade him to widen the radius of his generosity.[3]

The father has an excess of wealth to spare for this son, unlike for those suffering outside the gates of the estate. Despite the famine beyond the walls, a fattened calf is quickly slaughtered so that the family might celebrate in style.

Told from this perspective, the story charts a failure. The failure is neither in the son leaving his father's estate nor in his attempting to go back under different conditions, but rather in accepting his father's offer to be reintegrated back into the safe enclosure of the wealthy estate.

In this way, Brewin writes of how the story ends as it began: with a wealthy system walled off to the suffering surrounding it. The son left with a real possibility of breaking free from his past, of experiencing new ideas, and of returning home with a transformative message—one that would fundamentally challenge and change his family. But the act was ultimately impotent. It failed.

At the last moment he buckled and returned unchanged.

From the perspective of storytelling, this is a classic tragedy in that nothing changes. The end of the story is the same as the beginning, and everything is the way it used to be.

This story can be seen to mimic how old orders are threatened by subversive ideas and seek to seduce, coerce, or even threaten in order to expunge or domesticate the threat. For instance, it's not unusual for parents to fear the strange and unsettling ideas that their children might pick up at university, even attempting to send them to educational establishments that promise nothing but the replication of old values.

When a child goes to college there's always a threat that she might learn new ideas and come back with a very different way of viewing the world—a way that might threaten the fabric of the traditions that once comforted her.

It isn't surprising, then, that the father in this parable will hear nothing from his son, and instead silences him with the promise of wealth, status, and comfort. In this way, he's able to reintegrate his son back into the family, rather than have that family threatened.

His father might have proclaimed, "This son of mine was dead and is alive again," but for Brewin, the son, lying in his warm, safe bed, might have remembered the call of the road, the adventures, and friends and thought, "I was alive, but now I am dead."[4]

One of the ways that Brewin prepares his readers for this "dark" reading of the prodigal son is by contrasting it to the relationship that exists between Luke Skywalker and his father in *The Empire Strikes Back* and *Return of the Jedi*.[5]

In a classic scene from the former, Darth Vader reveals to an almost defeated Luke that he is in fact his father and wants him to join the empire where together they might rule the universe. Like the offer of the father in the prodigal story, this promise not only involves vast wealth and power, but would serve to mend a broken relationship and protect a family legacy.

But rather than succumbing to the offer, Luke remembers his friends and the oppression of the empire and enacts the classic revolutionary move by refusing to be reintegrated into the patriarchal system. He remains steadfast in the face of what must be a tempting offer, opting instead to remain with the rebel alliance and a thorn in the side of the empire.

Yet this act of rebellion is not ultimately one that stands *against* his father—for it eventually leads to his father's salvation.

We see this in *Return of the Jedi*, when Vader shows repentance for his past and kills the emperor. Where the prodigal son fails, Luke Skywalker succeeds. Where one father remains unchanged, the other is fundamentally transformed.

The subversive reading that Brewin puts forth gains its plausibility as one reads it against the story of Christ. For the wider gospel tells of another son in a similar family of three: a son who also leaves the safe confines of his father's wealthy estate, who also lives among animals for a time, and who also learns what it is to suffer.

The story of the prodigal and the story of Jesus both deal with a similar deadlock: to stay or return. But while one represents a failure in the face of the choice, the other represents a revolutionary success.

Like the story of the prodigal, the story of Jesus begins with a family that lives in a place of profound wealth, one that knows no poverty or need—a place devoid of suffering, decay, and death. Yet he, too, leaves his father's dwelling and enters a world that is all too familiar with these miseries. As Brewin notes, he, too, learns what it is to suffer:

> The story of the prodigal and the story of Jesus both deal with a similar deadlock: to stay or return.

> He came to earth from a place of comfort and experienced hunger, saw suffering, and knew pain. He came from a "kingdom of heaven" into an occupied territory, where he was excluded, disenfranchised, and, in all likelihood, economically exploited.[6]

Indeed, things get so bad that he's arrested, tortured, and made to undergo a slow and excruciating execution.

Like the prodigal, his father has not pursued him to bring him home. Like the prodigal, Jesus is left alone in a world that he chose to enter; and like the prodigal, Jesus can return at any time. At any moment, he could leave the cross and find a warm welcome back in the safe enclosure of the old order:

> Here was his temptation: to return to his father having changed nothing. He could accept his father's mantle with the old order still intact, and thus accept power and influence and the trappings of both. He could do that . . . or he could commit heresy against that old order, and reveal it for what it was: a form of social control which served to keep

a priestly elite well fed and very wealthy, while loading the poor with endless rules about what they could and could not do.[7]

As Jesus hangs on the cross, we the readers are left wondering what he might do. We are told that at any point he could cry out and his father's messengers would lift him off the cross, bandage his wounds, and bring him home.

Indeed, when his strength is all but gone and he hangs on to life with his bloodstained fingertips, he does cry out. But here is where the two stories most radically diverge, for this is not the cry of one saying "take me home."

Rather it is a cry that says, "Where are you? Why are you absent? Why have you left me to die?" This is not the tepid protest of the prodigal that melts away with the coldness that is banished by a warm robe.

This is an irreligious and resolute cry that emanates from insistent lips.

Now Christ is revealed as a paradigmatic trickster figure. Traditionally, tricksters are rebellious deities that break all the rules set down by gods and nature. While occasionally just playful and even malicious, the trickster archetype often employs rebellion, theft, and humor to subvert what we take to be sacred and to critique systems of inequality.

Christ here fits the description of the trickster in the way that he refuses to return to the wealthy enclosure of heaven and remains on the cross. It is a paradigmatic trickster move because of the way that it fundamentally disrupts our expectations and subverts the religious order.

This is demonstrated in the way that the curtain is ripped apart and the enclosed space of the Holy of Holies is exposed to the world. For Brewin,

> The rent curtain can be seen as Jesus "unmasking" his father God and exposing the reality behind the screen. In this reading, it is not that God was there and escaped; rather, the pulling back of this veil that separated common humanity from the "holy of holies" exposed as false the myth that God had even been there behind the curtain all along.[8]

In narrative terms this can be described as the conversion or self-saving of the father. Instead of the son going back to the safe estate, the father has to come out and experience the suffering world. The wealth hidden behind the curtain is dispersed in the world. Yet, from another perspective, this is a revelation of what has always already been the case: that the place of wealth was always a fiction and the true wealth of existence is to be found in the world. This is, then, the collapse of a two-world universe.

> Instead of the son going back to the safe estate, the father has to come out and experience the suffering world.

What we bear witness to in the story of Christ (as opposed to the prodigal) is the fundamental rejection of the sacred-object and, with it, the discovery of a new life committed to the world. This new life reflects the basic trickster move, namely a cutting against one's own system of meaning insofar as it inoculates itself from a commitment to the world. In the figure of Christ, then, we witness a true revolutionary: the one who cuts against one's own source for the sake of the world.

SECTION FOUR

BEHIND THE SCENES

CHAPTER 7

Outside the Magic Circle

This experience of working through the Pledge, Turn, and Prestige is a personal experience, but it is equally connected to wider concerns. Such a movement is a political happening, insofar as it transforms how we interact with the world.

This interconnection between the personal and political can be seen in the paradigmatic expression of conversion in Christianity. Namely the transformation of Saul on the road to Damascus:

> Meanwhile, Saul was still breathing out murderous threats against the Lord's disciples. He went to the high priest and asked him for letters to the synagogues in Damascus, so that if he found any there who belonged to the Way, whether men or women, he might take them as prisoners to Jerusalem. As he neared Damascus on his journey, suddenly a light from heaven flashed around him. He fell to the ground and heard a voice say to him, "Saul, Saul, why do you persecute me?"

"Who are you, Lord?" Saul asked.

"I am Jesus, whom you are persecuting," he replied. "Now get up and go into the city, and you will be told what you must do."

The men traveling with Saul stood there speechless; they heard the sound but did not see anyone. Saul got up from the ground, but when he opened his eyes he could see nothing. So they led him by the hand into Damascus. For three days he was blind, and did not eat or drink anything.

In Damascus there was a disciple named Ananias. The Lord called to him in a vision, "Ananias!"

"Yes, Lord," he answered.

The Lord told him, "Go to the house of Judas on Straight Street and ask for a man from Tarsus named Saul, for he is praying. In a vision he has seen a man named Ananias come and place his hands on him to restore his sight."

"Lord," Ananias answered, "I have heard many reports about this man and all the harm he has done to your holy people in Jerusalem. And he has come here with authority from the chief priests to arrest all who call on your name."

But the Lord said to Ananias, "Go! This man is my chosen instrument to proclaim my name to the Gentiles and their kings and to the people of Israel. I will show him how much he must suffer for my name."

Then Ananias went to the house and entered it. Placing his hands on Saul, he said, "Brother Saul, the Lord—Jesus, who appeared to you on the road as you were coming here—has sent me so that you may see again and be filled with the Holy Spirit." Immediately, something like scales fell from Saul's eyes, and he could see again. He got up and was baptized, and after taking some food, he regained his strength.[1]

We see here that Saul was utterly dedicated to persecuting a new religious sect that had grown out of Judaism. For Saul, this nascent group was a type of virus that had to be destroyed.

In this way, the Christian community functioned as a scapegoat for Saul: they were a thorn in the side of the existing religious structure that needed to be removed in order to ensure a harmonious and unified religious community.

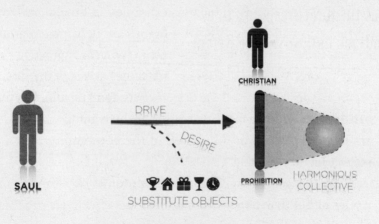

Saul's Obstacle

While Saul experiences the Christian community as an external growth that threatened the status quo, the community arose from *within* the religious structure that Saul represented. Like all such growths, the new community's very existence signified an issue within the religious structure of the day. In this sense, they were a *symptom*, i.e., the material manifestation, of an issue that was not being addressed.

This is not unlike the way that the Reformation functioned in relation to the Catholic Church of Luther's day, for his critique arose as a direct result of internal problems within the institution of the day and gained its power through the church's failure to face those problems.

> We see how a new religious or political community arises as the direct response to a deadlock in the existing system.

What we witness in such examples is how a new religious or political community (whether positive or negative) arises as the direct response to a deadlock in the existing system. They are attempts to resolve antagonisms that are being repressed or disavowed in the community they are responding to.

By treating the new Christian community as a foreign intruder rather than as a symptom, Saul was effectively avoiding a confrontation with the problems that had given rise to this group in the first place. Thus the peace that Saul might have imagined would result from the destruction of the Christians was a fantasy, a veil obscuring the truth of a problem within the existing religious order.

The imagined gridlock that Saul believed existed *because* of the movement actually helped to eclipse the very gridlock that *gave birth* to the movement.

What we are confronted with in the description of Saul's conversion is the way that he related to the Christian community as a scapegoat: he falsely perceived them to be the problem, when understanding that community would have actually helped to confront and overcome the problem.

To take a different example, we can reflect upon how homelessness in a society is generally seen as a problem that needs to be addressed, rather than being seen as a solution to a problem within the society. Without acknowledging this, any strategy aimed at removing homelessness is doomed to failure. For unless one understands how the homeless function in a society, then the real issue won't be addressed. If one is able to solve homelessness in a given society without addressing what gave rise to the problem, something else will simply take its place. Instead, the reason for the existence of the homeless must be assessed. In this way, the homeless become a voice of salvation to the very society that creates them.

Another example is the societal denial evidenced in the laws that protect people from being tortured for religious or political beliefs. The very existence of these laws signals a moral failing, in that only a society that creates the conditions for such torture needs to make a law that attempts to protect people from it. The idea of the oppressed and powerless being a prophetic voice to the system can be easily misunderstood. For it might seem to claim that an oppressed group is necessarily more moral than one that is not. This is obviously false when we consider how certain racist groups, for instance, are not given equal voice in a society. The point is not that they have a legitimate voice, but rather that their very existence signals a problem within the society that gave birth to them. Simply attempting to get rid of such a group will be ineffective if we do not strive to understand and address the situation that enabled them to gain a foothold.

When considering Saul's conversion, we see a dramatic example of how the position of the outsiders offers a call to transformation. In the narrative, those he believed to be damned were suddenly revealed as the path to salvation. On the road to Damascus, he heeds a voice that informs him that he is in fact persecuting God. His conversion mimics the theological meaning of the Crucifixion, for Christ is treated as a scapegoat who turns out to be the way of salvation.

This is where the theological conservative comes closest to the radical position, for the conservative also associates Christ with the torn curtain of the temple, but for very different reasons. While the conservative reads Christ as the curtain who is "torn" so that we can gain what lies on the other side, the radical interpretation sees Christ as the curtain that, when torn, reveals the emptiness of what lies on the other side. Here the conservative interpretation is structurally the same as that of the rabble gathered at the trial of Jesus, with the exception that for the rabble, Jesus is the obstacle that must be abolished to fulfill the law, while for the conservative, Jesus is the lamb that must be sacrificed to fulfill it.

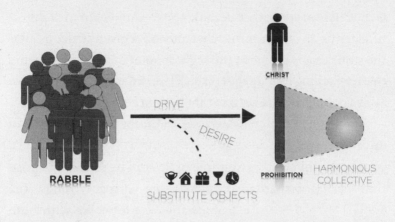

Christ the Scapegoat

In contrast, the radical reading claims that the very act of scapegoating is a fundamental failure, but a failure that opens up a victory. For it is when we realize that the destruction of the scapegoat is powerless to help that we can realize that listening to the scapegoat is where the transformation lies.

In this radical reading of Christ's crucifixion, it is only after Christ has been killed that we realize the failure of our scapegoating and the reality that what we thought we needed to destroy in order to get to the sacred was in fact sacred. This is captured powerfully in the response of the Roman centurion who proclaims, "Surely this was the son of God," once Jesus has died.[2]

Here the centurion symbolically stands in for the one who realizes that the obstacle was in fact the way.

This can help us understand why one of the terms for Christ

is the rejected stone that became the capstone. For in architectural terms, the capstone is what anchors a given structure; it is the stone that is placed at the highest point in an arch to ensure that everything else stays in place. Here the stone that is thrown away is revealed as the stone that is most central.

The logic of the cross exposes the scapegoat as the way of salvation.

Another interesting example of this can be seen in the position that the Samaritan is given in the Gospel writings. The Samaritans were a people with both Jewish and pagan ancestry and who diverged somewhat from the practices of mainstream Judaism. They were largely disliked and viewed with suspicion by the religious establishment of the day. Indeed, rather than pass through Samaritan territory, many Jews who were traveling between Judea and Galilee would take a much longer route to get to their destination.

> The logic of the cross exposes the scapegoat as the way of salvation.

It's clear that the importance Jesus placed on the Samaritans was not related to their particular beliefs and practices (which he doesn't mention), but rather to their lowly position within the religious system of the day. The parable of a Samaritan who helps someone on the side of the road is a clear challenge to the way the Samaritans were being scapegoated. In this parable, the Samaritan is placed in the position of the godly act, thus turning the dominant prejudice of the day on its head.

It is on the road to Damascus that we see this insight taking place in the life of Saul. In a brief moment, he realizes that the group he's persecuting is not what stands in the way of his salvation, but is the very path to salvation.

On his way to Damascus he's directly confronted with his own violence devoid of any sacred justification. He experiences the persecuted community as a prophetic voice addressed to him, and he heeds the message.

In an act of profound grace, the traumatized Saul is welcomed in and cared for by one of the very people he has been seeking to destroy. Then, when he is better, he demonstrates the reality of his transformation by committing himself to a very different mission. He changes his name to Paul, and he dedicates himself to the formation of a new type of community—one that questions the final legitimacy of a religious identity or confessional tradition. He dedicated himself to a community of *neither/nor*—neither Jew nor Gentile, neither slave nor free, neither male nor female.[3] By breaking down these tribal identities, he drains scapegoating of its power. This is not to say that Paul wasn't a man of his times with views that reflect those of his day, but his lasting insight was one of a new type of community that would cut against the various tribal identities in operation at the time. A vision that has as much power and significance for us now as it did then.

It is this disturbing, disruptive, and destabilizing idea of neither/nor that has been domesticated and effectively silenced in the church, arising only on the edges of the religious tradition in mystics like Meister Eckhart (who was accused of heresy) and Marguerite Porete (who was burned at the stake).

Paul's conversion offers us a glimpse of what it might mean to form communities of practice where the scapegoat is smashed and where we exorcise the demonic power of exclusionary systems—communities where we learn what it might look like to embrace equality, solidarity, and universal emancipation.

This new community envisaged by Paul is not some alternative to what already exists, but rather is a vision that can be adopted by already existing communities. If it were as simple as the idea of creating some new group, this would itself become its own new tradition that would need to be challenged. This idea of the neither/nor should be approached as a way of revolutionizing already existing communities.

The attempt to open already existing communities to what they exclude might well lead to new groups—that is, if the attempt is rejected—but it might also lead to the transformation of what already is.

While a new grouping grew out of Paul's mission—the Christian Church—the point of neither/nor collectives is not to create a new ideological cult, but to break open already existing ideological systems.

By taking this approach to Paul, we gain a picture of what it might be like to found a community that is not in submission to its political, cultural, and religious markers. Of course, new communities will arise out of old ones, and no community will ever be free of bias, conflict, and prejudices. But the possibility is held out for communities that are willing and able to challenge themselves, face their internal conflicts, and strive to better enact liberation.

A King Is a King Because We Treat Him as One

Such a collective, as we have already mentioned, wrestles with the ideological systems it is immersed in. The demand to wrestle with God as a trickster becomes the model for how we must wrestle with any order that justifies us and holds everything in place.

Ideology is the justification of an actual state of affairs that polices the boundaries between what is considered pure and impure, good and bad, inside and outside. At the time of Paul the system that held sway broadly defined people in terms of one's identity as a Jew or a Gentile, a male or female, a slave or a free person. Each of these identities carried with it certain roles and responsibilities, with some being valued more highly than others.

The system was taken to be divinely established, and so to question it was not simply to debate the political and religious structure, but to rebel against the laws of nature and the will of God. Even if people didn't actually believe in God or natural law, the population acted as if it were true—either through fear, custom, self-preservation, or profit. It is this bodily commitment to a social order that manifests ideology at its zero level—as a system that continues to operate even among those who do not intellectually endorse it.

> To question the system was not simply to debate the political and religious structure, but to rebel against the laws of nature and the will of God.

We can see how this operates in the HBO series *Game of Thrones*, for here we witness various characters cynically engaging with the system of power. One of the few figures who actually appeared to believe in the system was King Joffrey, a psychotic figure who inscribed the immaterial order into his subjectivity: believing that he was in fact a king rather than a mere boy filling the role of a king. The fact that few of the characters are true believers in the system is captured in the very name *Game of Thrones*.

What we are faced with in the conversion of Saul is the possibility of a community dedicated to the undermining of systems that would seek to enshrine inequality. When Paul writes of a community where there is no Jew or Gentile, male or female, slave or free, he is describing a collective where these identities are drained of their operative power and where everyone has equal access to the universal. This is not a new system, but rather a way of living out the system that one already inhabits. Paul introduces a truly shattering alternative to the system of his day, in which everything was ordered in strict hierarchies. He directly connects this new approach with Christ crucified. For Crucifixion describes one who was stripped of all identity. To be crucified meant to be robbed of one's political and religious status. The person being executed was no longer a citizen and was considered cursed of God. Thus to identify with someone on a cross was to identify with someone robbed of identity.

To be "crucified with Christ" thus speaks of a breaking of strict identity markers. This doesn't mean that people now no longer have identities, but they now hold them in such a way that they no longer define the scope and limitations of their lives. A new conflict arises, not between different groups, but between those who are open to change and those who hold stubbornly to their tribal identities.

The radical church finds itself *in* the world and yet no longer *of* it. It remains part of a wider society, with all of its hierarchies, and yet it fundamentally questions these hierarchies.

Holy Crap

Paul describes this new community as made up of those who are the "trash of the world."[4] In his book *Signs of Emergence*, Kester Brewin explores how trash can be described as "matter out of place." It is that which is in our world and yet which disturbs it, that which seems out of place within it.

Interestingly, this idea of something that inhabits the world while not part of that world can describe how the holy inhabits space—that which is *wholly other*, yet *in our midst*.

It is in his definition of the Christ collective as the trash of the world that Paul forms a fascinating *coincidentia oppositorum* (coincidence of opposites), for here the trash and the holy become indistinguishable from each other. The trash *of* the world becomes the site of holiness *in* the world—the stone that we reject becomes the capstone.

What we learn here is that the boundaries between pure and impure are placed into question and the outside becomes the inside—something that we even see played out in the doctrine that seems most resistant to such ideas: predestination. For the Scriptures name only one man predestined for the bowels of hell, and that is Jesus. Here the outside is seen as the very place Christ enters. Thus the radical collective is found in those who identify as the outsiders, as those who are nothing and nobodies: this is the meaning of Christ's descent into hell.

In the idea of the trash of the world, we see that the idea of the "villains of all nations"—the pirates that we looked at previously—expands and takes on cosmic significance; the rejected become synonymous with the sacred.

Many religious communities are either offensive in all the wrong ways (because of reactionary stands on sexuality, race, and politics) or profoundly inoffensive and anemic (offering a feel-good, self-help prosperity preaching). But Paul opens up the idea of a place that is offensive in all the right ways, saying that those who congratulate themselves for being inside are actually outside and those who are on the outside are actually inside.

> The radical community is thus the place that displaces us, the place that challenges us to be in the world but not of it.

The radical community is thus the place that displaces us, the place that challenges us to be in the world but not of it, to embrace the oppressed and be transformed by them.

Religious Belief Requires Unbelief

What we see in this reading of Paul's conversion is a move from a religious worldview to a faith that embraces the world regardless of worldview. We see the formation of groups that constantly question, critique, and undermine their own belief systems, in light of a call to enact greater liberation and democracy.

Yet if this is the case, then the question must be asked as to why parts of the biblical text seem so disparaging of unbelief.

If belief, as we are exploring here, were a problem, then why would its opposite be seen as bad in the biblical text?

The answer perhaps lies in the way that a certain form of unbelief is not actually opposed to belief, but rather acts as one of the mechanisms that enables belief to sustain itself.

It is all too common for people to think that the problem with unbelief is that it stands in opposition to belief—that it prevents us *from* believing more fully. However, the problem with unbelief lies precisely in the opposing position: it supports and sustains belief.

That is, *it enables us to continue in our belief.*

In my early twenties, I witnessed this reality firsthand when I attended a church service in which the speaker gave an impassioned sermon on the subject of supernatural healing. After the talk, a person sitting across from me tripped when he was getting up and seriously damaged his arm. Inspired by what I'd just heard, I brought him to the side of the room and started to pray for healing.

As I prayed, someone found the speaker and brought him over. I asked the speaker (who also happened to be a doctor) to pray with us, but instead, he examined the arm and told us that we had to get him to the hospital.

This is not something I had even contemplated. I'd just heard a sermon about healing and believed it. It was the person who preached the sermon who didn't believe. His own belief was sustained by an underlying unbelief. In other words, his intellectual affirmation of healing helped him psychologically, yet he held that affirmation at arm's length in terms of his lived practice.

In fundamentalist communities, the explicit beliefs of the community can continue to exist precisely because they are supported by a disavowed unbelief. For instance, a congregation might affirm the idea that if you show no doubt, God will always bring healing, or that we will be much better off in the next life than this one, or that our loved ones who do not express a belief in Jesus are going to an unending punishment. Yet in such communities, most still call the ambulance if their loved one is having a seizure, they don't shoot their children to hasten their journey to heaven, and they don't act as one would who knew that most of his friends were on the verge of entering a hell of unending torture.

Their belief is a fantasy that is supported by a repressed unbelief.

Because of this carefully concealed distance between a person's claims and her actual stance, it is actually the "full believer" who is more of a threat to Fundamentalist and conservative communities than the one who claims that those communities believe too much. It is precisely the full believer who best exposes the Fundamentalist fantasy as a fantasy. For example, consider the situation where a child dies as the direct result of a parent who has complete belief in healing and thus *doesn't* call an ambulance. In such cases, the impotence of the Fundamentalist system is glimpsed in the very act of the one who most fully affirms it. The parents were supposed to not really believe what was being said from the pulpit. In relation to the idea explored earlier, they were supposed to know that this was a belief that should be quietly transgressed.

Within a Fundamentalist community, certain religion beliefs continue to function the way they do only because they are *not* believed at a material level: because unbelief is in operation.

It's Not That You Believe Too Much— You Don't Believe Enough

Fundamentalist communities are not threatened by the liberal claim that they believe too much, for this plays into the very fantasy that sustains them. The threatening move in such communities lies in the other direction: in exposing how they don't believe enough. Why? Because it is only as they fully accept their beliefs without unbelief that they are faced with the powerlessness and even horror of those beliefs. It is only then that the beliefs themselves might crumble into dust.

Many of the people who move beyond Fundamentalist communities are not the ones who avoid taking it seriously, but precisely those who take it more seriously than the majority. It is these individuals who are confronted with the true horror of what they affirm. In contrast, the ones who continue in a mode of disavowed disbelief are the ones who find it easier to stay in Fundamentalist communities because they're able to pay lip service to the dogmas of the church without really experiencing their impotence. The problem with unbelief here is precisely that it enables people to keep believing.

This relation between belief and unbelief is what we see in Paul's understanding of Law and sin: where the Law appears to be the opposite of sin but actually gives sin its libidinal support.

Unfortunately, it's often the case that by the time someone takes his beliefs absolutely seriously and discovers their impotence, it's too difficult for him to leave. This is most obvious among religious leaders who have jobs within their institutions. For often they find the limits of their beliefs only when they are wholly dependent on their church for material support. Hence it becomes harder to leave at the very point when they are most disillusioned.

This is why it is often true that the closer we get to the inner circle of the church the more we find cynicism, hypocrisy, and repression. A layperson can avoid a confrontation with the impotence of her beliefs by imagining that if only she were more involved, things would be better. But those who are the most involved often have no fantasy left to sustain them. They've been to the center, and they've discovered that the center is no better than the edges. But now they rely on that center for support, so they give themselves to support it.

I'm Not Disagreeing with You; I'm Disagreeing with Myself

Removing our unbelief is not then what frees our religious belief to exist unfettered. Rather, religious belief begins to crumble at the very point when *unbelief* is removed. Unbelief is the problem, not because it stops us from believing too much, but because it helps us continue to believe unabated. An insidious unbelief allows communities to get the psychological pleasure from the beliefs they hold without having to actually confront the horror of fully affirming them in a material way.

This is why people who have beliefs and practices that are foreign to such communities can be so threatening. It is not because of their "otherness" as such, but because of the way their otherness threatens to expose the otherness that already exists within the community. In short, we can be faced with our own repressed skepticism when we see it expressed in another person.

Take the example of a married couple talking to someone who does not believe in the institution of marriage. If the couple becomes deeply agitated and angered by what the other person is saying (or visa versa), it can begin to look as if the disagreement signals something other than a mere difference of opinion. The people being agitated start to look as if they are covering over some internal doubts of their own by needing to aggressively defend their position. The conflict between the two groups becomes a distraction from the deeper conflict that is nestled *within* the antagonized party. In other words, the inner antagonism that arises from a person's own repressed doubts is directed *outward*, thus obscuring the true source of the conflict: a conflict existing due to a clash between what the person professes as true and the repressed doubts he has.

CHAPTER 8

Restaging the Trick

Thus far we have looked at Christianity as the enactment of something structurally similar to what we witness in a magic trick, a trick that transforms the very texture and quality of our life. However, instead of a sleight of hand, this "magic trick" involves a slight shift in perspective in which fullness of life is no longer sought in a distant realm, but rather is found in the very midst of our lives.

This change in perspective means that heaven and earth are no longer seen as separate, but the sacred and profane are fused, and the pursuit of a single fruit-bearing tree is replaced with the vision of an abundant world ready for harvest.

Sadly, however, it can seem that one of the institutions most dedicated to preventing this experience is the contemporary church. In the hands of the pious professionals, "God" is presented as nothing less than an object that promises satisfaction and certainty. For a small cost, they hand out placebos, promising that they will protect against the experience that life is difficult and that we don't know the answers.

The Living Idol

One of the ways that the church attempts to protect people from the loss of the sacred-object is through a direct affirmation that it exists and that we already have it. We see this in fundamentalist settings, where it is directly affirmed that they are in relationship with the one who makes all things new. The songs and sermons all affirm a joyous reality that guests are welcomed to experience for themselves through the altar call.

The question one must ask, however, concerns how much this is actually believed by the majority of those leading and attending such communities.

In order to approach an answer, let us reflect upon how language functions in the following story about an Englishman, a Scotsman, and an Irishman who are training to join the Special Forces.

After passing all the preliminary tests, the three men are brought to an isolated house in the countryside. The Englishman is called first and enters a room where his sergeant sits behind a desk. The sergeant places a gun full of blanks on the table and says, "We've got to make sure that you're ready to do whatever it takes. I need you to pick up this gun, go into the next room, and kill whoever is in there."

The Englishman nods silently, picks up the gun, and goes into the other room. Five minutes pass before he comes out, white as a sheet. "My best friend's in there. I just can't do it."

Next the Scotsman is called in and given the same speech. Like the Englishman, he, too, picks up the gun and walks into the room. This time ten minutes pass before a shot rings out.

The Scotsman comes out of the room, shaking like a leaf. "My best friend was in there," he says, "but I knew you wouldn't have put live rounds in the gun, so I pulled the trigger."

Finally the Irishman is called in. Again, the sergeant tells him to pick up the gun and kill whoever is in the next room. The Irishman picks up the weapon and walks through the door. After a few minutes, the sergeant hears a shot quickly followed by a scream and the sound of smashing glass. The Irishman then reemerges panting heavily. "Some idiot put blanks in the gun," he shouts. "So I had to use a chair."

While one might think that the Irishman best represents what we see in Fundamentalism, it is rather the Scotsman. For the Scotsman is the one who hears the manifest message (kill the guy), but who understands and obeys the implicit content of that message (don't kill the guy).

In contrast, the Irishman is engaged in a type of psychotic relation to language in which the manifest message is embraced without taking into consideration the implicit demand to transgress the order.

The relation of the Irishman to language is akin to what we see in the typical gender stereotype of TV sitcoms where a woman talks to a man about how awful her day was (how her boss is out to get her and how nobody seems to care), only to be told by the man that she is being unreasonable. In these scenarios the man is presented as the voice of reason, telling her to see things from the other person's perspective and realize that she isn't being persecuted. While this fits within what seems like a standard sexist trope (the woman being unreasonable and the man being reasonable), such a scenario can be read in the opposite way.

The assumption of the man is that the woman's empirically unreasonable discourse is actually communicating only what it explicitly says. In this way, the man is blind to what is likely to be a much richer mode of communication, one that he can't see because of his literalism. In such a situation, it is perfectly possible that the woman is simply speaking out her very real frustrations. The point is that the woman may already know full well that things are not the way that she has subjectively expressed them and that her point in speaking is to simply come to a place where she can better accept that truth.

In other words, the man misunderstands the nature of the discourse and naïvely points out something the woman is already aware of.

The same logic often plays out if we break up with someone and express our anger to a friend, only to be told to see things from the other person's perspective. In response, we could say to our friend, "I know full well that I treated her badly, that I was emotionally unavailable and much more, but I need to be able to say all of this so I can come to accept it."

> What we most often confront in fundamentalist and conservative settings is not the "full believer," but rather the "ironic believer."

Without a space where we can be "unreasonable," we might never get to the point where we let negative emotions go and learn to move on.

As we have already explored, what we most often confront in fundamentalist and conservative settings is not the "full believer" (the Irishman), but rather the "ironic believer" (the Scotsman).

It's not, then, that the Fundamentalist affirms that "God" (as the sacred-object) is alive. It's that she subjectively claims this "God" is alive, while demonstrating her unbelief in this "God" through her actions. While being affirmed as alive, this idol is already dead. A truth that will be evidenced in all manner of symptoms.

The Unconscious Idol

In contrast to fundamentalist and conservative churches, more liberal and progressive communities tend to subjectively question the idea of God as the garniture of certainty and satisfaction. Someone in a liberal community might, for example, affirm the mystery of God and/or the limits of human understanding in order to find a place for doubt and unknowing.

However, while fundamentalist and conservative churches tend to encourage their congregants to use their *beliefs* to avoid a confrontation with the trauma of unknowing and facing lack, the liberal communities tend to encourage a repression of that trauma through their *liturgical structure*. While those in more liberal and progressive circles would generally reject the idea that "God" protects us from difficulties and doubt, their hymns, prayers, and creeds often affirm those very ideas. The consolation isn't in the actual beliefs but rather is imbedded in the practices.

Just as fundamentalist communities offer a security blanket

through their belief, the liberal and progressive communities are able to do so through their liturgical affirmations. Prayer, sermons, hymns, and rituals effectively serve to prop up the very system that is intellectually questioned. It would be hard to turn to a random page in any hymnbook and find something that did not affirm a view of God that would be denied by many of the people singing.

> Just as fundamentalist communities offer a security blanket through their belief, the liberal and progressive communities are able to do so through their liturgical affirmations.

It's like the parent who doesn't believe in the tooth fairy but enjoys the effects of the belief through the ritual of removing the tooth from under her child's pillow and replacing it with money.

The problem, however, is that this keeps us from fully entering into the Prestige of faith. It is simply a more advanced way of protecting ourselves from the trauma of the Turn and staying at the level of the Pledge.

By using rituals as a way of cradling our belief, we outsource our Fundamentalism and enlist a third party to protect us from the trauma of losing the sacred-object.

The Dead Idol

In contrast to the above ways of psychologically avoiding a confrontation with the traumatic Turn of Christianity, which we can call the first and second naïveté, the radical position seeks to confront us with the task of *abolishing the naïveté in both its forms.*

This does not mean that the radical approach sets up an alternative structure that embraces the death of the sacred-object, but rather that it seeks to bring to the surface the ways in which that death is already dimly perceived, yet denied, in already existing confessional systems.

The point then is to help break the false distinction between the idea that there are those who are whole and those who have a lack. For the true distinction is between those who hide their lack under the fiction of wholeness *and those who are able to embrace it.*

This requires a reinterpretation of the religious journey that is generally stated as having three movements: a state of original blessing, followed by a fall, and culminating in redemption.

This first stage of original blessing can be described as the claim that there was once a state of equilibrium, wholeness, and fulfillment. Depending on whom you talk to, this state might lie in childhood, in a past relationship, in some cultural golden era, or in a kind of pre-Fall paradise.

It is then said that something disturbed this peace. This is said to articulate our current state, a state in which there is a profound disruption of the harmony that once existed. Like original Blessing, this idea of the Fall has its religious and secular expressions: it might be described in terms of a broken relationship, ill health, a general melancholy, or spiritual oppression.

Finally there is Redemption. Like the others, this promise takes various forms, but it always involves the articulation of a future in which the balance, order, and harmony that we have lost will be restored.

However powerful as this description can be, the truth is a little different. Instead, we start out with a sense of fall (the loss of the sacred-object) that causes us to imagine a prior state of blessing (where we once had it), which in turn encourages us to long for a future redemption (where we will have it again).

It is the three-part frame of Blessing, Fall, and Redemption that the radical church must expose as problematic. To understand how the documentary *Kumaré* directed by Vikram Gandhi is useful, *Kumaré* follows Vikram Gandhi as he transforms himself into a fictional guru from a nonexistent village in India. As part of this deception, he takes on an Indian accent, grows a long beard, and carries a staff. He then makes up a religious philosophy and goes to Arizona to spread his message.

Gandhi's stated motivation for engaging in this fiction lies in his suspicion that the whole industry of spiritual leaders is itself a form of fiction, that individuals set themselves up as enlightened for less-than-enlightened reasons (such as a desire for money or power).

Without much trouble, he finds that he's able to form a religion and develop a small but loyal following among a variety of people who are struggling with different issues.

To make matters more interesting, he even hints at the scam

by telling his followers that he is not what he appears to be, that he is a fake, and that they need to take responsibility for their own lives. This message, however, is affirmed by his followers in a way that undermines the content, for they remain utterly committed to him as their guru.

For the scam to be exposed, a more radical step is required, which is exactly what we witness at the end of *Kumaré*, when Gandhi fully confronts his followers with the truth. Those who believed him to be a guru were gathered in a room and then watched as he walked in dressed in normal clothes, without the beard, staff, or fake accent. Only at this point did they discover the truth: that he was not a great religious leader.

In this moment, those who followed him were confronted directly with the loss of the sacred-object. Yet while this was shocking, the majority of those gathered experienced this great unveiling in a positive way. Despite the deception, these individuals were now free from this religious structure they had participated in. They had made positive changes in their lives because of it, but now they were able to embrace those changes without needing the structure itself.

Thus one might want to say that it was in Gandhi's very confession of being a fake guru that he momentarily expressed what it might mean to be a real one.

This divestment of power is what a community, which is seeking to remain true to the event within Christianity, should attempt to emulate. People will come to the community for answers and yet gradually come to realize that the answers are not there. They will find, instead, a group of people attempting to live well amid the loss of the perfect answer.

This is not the liberal move of simply telling people that the structure is powerless while keeping the structure in place. As we see in the documentary, as long as the guru keeps up with his made-up rituals, his revelation that he is powerless has no operative power.

The impotence of this move is expressed well in a story Derrida once used concerning two high-ranking religious leaders who meet in a place of worship. When the first man enters the building, he goes up to the altar, bows, and says, "I am nothing but dust from the earth."

When the second man enters, he approaches the altar, gets onto his knees, and says, "Here I am, nothing but dust."

There also happens to be a caretaker in the room, quietly mopping the floor as the two religious figures talk. When he is finished, he, too, goes up to the altar. He kneels before it and says, "Dust I am, and to dust I shall return."

At this, one of the religious leaders turns to the other in disgust and cries out, "Who does he think he is, claiming he's dust!"

What we witness here is that when these religious leaders claim to be dust, they say it in a way that affirms their substance as more than dust. The claim is undermined by the very way that the claim is held.

The issue is that the religious structure must embody the message of its own comic nature. Those who say that the church is powerless to fix us are right—and the church itself should be the place that reveals this reality most powerfully. Like *Kumaré,* the church reveals that it has no mystical power to grant us what will make us whole and that what we have, instead, is each other.

CHAPTER 9

The Vanishing Priest

Radical liturgy is dedicated to the formation of spaces in which we actively confront our own lack in order to rob that lack of its sting. This failure to look at the lack is not an explicitly religious problem, it is equally a secular one, and as such, atheism itself can be held as a security blanket.

This can seem counterintuitive in that atheism is not used to affirm some belief, but rather to reject it. It's easy to see how a system of belief can operate as a security blanket, but it's not so easy to see how a rejection of belief can operate as such. Yet it was the philosopher Friedrich Nietzsche who, at the twilight of the nineteenth century, saw that atheism could function much like a religion. This is most clearly seen in his famous parable of the madman who proclaims that God is dead to a group of people who don't believe in God; i.e., the madman is not addressing theists, but atheists. He goes on to chastise them for not understanding their own position, for being unable to experience what they affirm.

The madman is telling them what they seem to already

know, namely that God is dead as an anchoring point in their lives, that this God is an idea whose time has passed: *but he's accusing them of not knowing it.*

He compares it to the relationship of thunder to lightning. After the lightning has struck, the rumbling sound of the thunder lags behind. The people whom the madman addresses may believe that God is dead, but they haven't felt it yet. Elsewhere Nietzsche refers to an old myth about the shadow of the Buddha remaining on a cave wall after the Buddha had died. The argument here can be broadly read as claiming that the "death of God" (the philosophical name for the theological death of the sacred-object) is not itself fully accomplished in the atheism that would seem to proclaim it.

It is precisely here that radical theology comes in with its critique that the atheism we know today (i.e., "New Atheism") has not gone too far in its religious critique, but rather that it hasn't gone far enough: that it is still caught beneath the shadow of the idolatrous God that it thinks it has cast aside.

More than this, it is here that the radical approach draws out how the subversive and scandalous heart of Christianity invites us to take the next step and experience this death in the very core of our being. An experience that is open to those who are theists, atheists, and agnostics. Radical theology is thus not following in the footsteps of religious apologists, who wish to step back from New Atheism, but rather seeks to take a step further.

God, You Gotta Love Him

As we've noted, one of the ways that the event sheltered in the name of Christianity has been obscured is in the obsession with belief. Whether it's an interfaith dialogue or a debate between a theist and an atheist, the intellectual affirmations of each party are placed at the forefront of the discussion as having central importance.

The problem here, however, is that it would be perfectly possible to change the entire content of our beliefs without altering the way our beliefs function.

Take the example of someone who identifies as an evangelical Christian and for whom that belief acts as a type of emotional crutch. Let us imagine this person growing up in an overtly religious environment in which evangelical belief functioned primarily as a means of defining oneself over and against others.

> It would be perfectly possible to change the entire content of our beliefs without altering the way our beliefs function.

If this belief is later rejected in favor of some other religious or political system, it might look like a fundamental change has taken place. However, at a structural level, these different beliefs will operate in broadly the same way as the old ones. Regardless of which view might provide a more accurate description of reality, we discover that the new set of beliefs also functions as a security blanket, a tribal identity, and a means of coping with the sense of cosmic insecurity.

Christianity, as a *religious* system, does not aim to transform the way we believe, but strives to mold and shape the content of our beliefs. What is judged here to be of prime importance is the actual belief that one affirms. So those who agree are deemed "saved," and those who disagree are at best heretics, or at worst "lost."

Take the example of a church pastor who preaches a sermon about how much God hates us. In the aftermath of this, it would be likely that lots of religious believers would raise their voice to assure people that God really loves everyone. Indeed, if a religious leader knew someone who took such a message to heart, she might approach that person and attempt to find out exactly why. It's not hard to imagine that a person who believes that God hates him might be struggling with a deep sense of self-hatred or guilt that might be worked through with the right type of care.

There is no problem with trying to ascertain why someone would resonate with the idea of divine hatred; the problem is when we only apply such a therapeutic practice to those people we deem to hold negative beliefs. A pastor should also approach those who resonate with the message that God loves them and ask why. For there could well be unhealthy reasons why this message of divine love relates to them. Take the quip that circled around Europe during the Iraq war: "Americans, you gotta love them—otherwise they'll bomb you."

The phrase gets its humor from turning the assumption that the love is a gift into the revelation that the love is actually a demand.

When we apply this to the idea of someone affirming God's love, the question remains as to how this belief functions. For it's perfectly possible that the person's explicit claim, "God, you gotta love him," has, at a disavowed level, the threat "otherwise he'll burn you."

If we concentrate on the level of manifest belief and fail to look at how the belief functions, we'll never know what motivates and sustains it. Not that this is easy to work out. The way our beliefs function can be oblique, not just to other people, but more fundamentally, to ourselves.

It is only through deep and sustained reflection that we might begin to see what lies beneath the statement. In doing this, we may discover that behind the seeming free expression there is actually a traumatic memory, such as being told at a young age that God will punish anyone who doesn't love him.

The point is that even when people change their beliefs, they often do so as a way of *preserving* the very same role that the former beliefs played (just as changing one high-fat food for another doesn't change the fact that you are eating a high-fat diet). At a superficial level, we could change our beliefs many times over without substantially challenging the way in which we hold those beliefs.

The focus on "correcting" a religious belief that we think is incorrect thus obscures the more important and difficult task of discovering *why* a particular belief is held in the first place and how it *functions* in our lives.

When we situate the question of faith at the level of the *how* rather than the *what*, the question regarding what it means to believe in God is transformed. In properly theological terms, the question is no longer about the existence or inexistence of some being, but rather about whether or not one is responding to a call that throws him into a deep concern and care for the world. This approach is not concerned with whether we label ourselves theist, atheist, or agnostic. Indeed, such a perspective allows us to open ourselves up to the possibility that the boundaries that supposedly separate these different positions are in fact fluid.

Despite the territorial divisions that separate theists from atheists, many of us are very aware that we dwell on the border—occasionally passing from one side to the other or finding ourselves in a liminal space that doesn't quite belong to any side.

Whether it's a church leader who finds herself embarrassed by what she preaches, a humanist who sings hymns with the conviction of a saint, a theist who finds the idea of God absurd, or an atheist who secretly prays—the walls that separate can often be more permeable than we might like to admit.

If we move away from the importance of what we believe to questions concerning how our belief functions, then it's easier for us to acknowledge that there might be some of the theist, the atheist, and the agnostic in each of us, even though one might take precedence over the others.

The Art of Disruption

One of the ways we can begin to uncover how our belief functions is to engage in practices that disrupt, disturb, surprise, and confront us—practices that help bring to light the things that the individual or community have repressed.

No discourse is immune from being used as a protection mechanism, and thus, any system can become a type of enclosure that prevents us from being shocked by our own being and disturbed by our own acts. Indeed, as New Atheism makes clear, even a discourse that champions nonbelief can fall into this trap.

The point is not to try and find a certain theological language that is somehow "correct," but rather to encourage a form of *dialectic movement* in those who participate in the rituals and practices of the radical church.

The way dialectic movement functions can be seen in the therapeutic example of a young man in analysis who described his attachment to a particular woman in terms of a drug addiction. During a session, he spoke of how he sought the high of the connection with her, even though these connections were inevitably followed by long, dark lows. As the session ended, the therapist simply asked if the young man was in fact an addict who was seeking the *lows* rather than the highs.

This rhetorical question had the effect of opening up a new line of thought in the analysand (the one undergoing analysis), one that enabled him to explore the idea that he might get something out of his depression and might even be seeking it out in some unconscious way.

The question asked by the analyst in this session is an example of how a type of dialectic movement might be encouraged, a movement that can shake an individual out of a certain groove of thought by exposing something unsaid within it.

In a subtle way, the analyst was able to present an idea that uncovered a complex relation between pleasure and pain in the analysand that he was previously unaware of. In this brief moment the analysand was surprised by himself and disturbed in a fruitful way.

This is a dialectic move precisely because the negation is already a *negation of negation*. For when the question "Are you actually seeking the low" is posed, there is an implication that the individual might be seeking the low *because* that is where the real high is. In dialectic terms it works like this:

AFFIRMATION: I'm seeking the high.

NEGATION: I'm seeking the low.

NEGATION OF NEGATION: I'm seeking the low because I get some kind of high from it.

From this insight, the analysand might be more able to self-interrogate regarding why he holds on to painful situations.

This example can help us understand one of the fundamental opening moves of churches that seek to live out this type of dialectic subversion.

Such groups attempt to provoke a type of dialectic dynamic that uncovers the hidden shadows of the conscious affirmations in a given group—all of which serve to surprise the community with its own repressed content. They attempt to cultivate an inherently subversive set of practices that continually try to negate the affirmation of a particular group, regardless of what that affirmation is—practices that I have elsewhere called Transformance Art.

Because of the subversive nature of Transformance Art, there needs to be a context that is inviting, encouraging, and supportive; for like therapy, the journey can be a painful one.

Agents of Decay

The challenge of Transformance Art lies not in getting people to admit the impotence of their idols, but in getting them to admit that they *already know this impotence in some way*. As such the radical church can be described as a *putrid agent* dedicated to encouraging the decay of that which we already know is dead.

The term *decay* is important for a couple of reasons. First, because exposure to decay is more visceral than exposure to death. The decay of those we love can be more traumatic to us than their death. Not because the decay is worse than the death, but because decay confronts us more fully with the *reality* of the death.

Decay confronts us more fully with the *reality* of the death.

It is the thunder that follows the lightning.

Consider how dead bodies are preserved and put on display in some cultures before being buried or cremated. The process of embalming ensures that the signs of decay are concealed. This helps to protect loved ones from a visceral encounter with the horror of the loss.

Indeed, the bodies of some political leaders have been preserved and put on extended public view in a dead but preserved state. Leaders such as Vladimir Lenin, Joseph Stalin, Mao Zedong, and Kim Jong-il have all been put on display in this way. The dead body thus effectively remains as a symbolic reminder of the regimes they sustained. While the political figure is no more, the dead body communicates that the regime continues to exert its power. In the example of Communist Russia, it was only when the Stalinist regime began to actually crumble that Stalin's body was finally removed from Lenin's tomb in Red Square and allowed to rot.

In relation to those we love, the recognition of their decay can be the very thing from which we wish to protect ourselves. For instance, the act of keeping the room of a dead child exactly as it was while the child was living can provide a certain needed buffer from the horror of the loss, allowing for a temporary respite from the agony of the tragedy. This can be an important interim act, but if the room is never touched, it can gradually become something that prevents the parents from fully coming to terms with the loss.

This is why the radical tradition attempts to enact the decay of the sacred-object rather than simply acknowledge its death. For only when decay occurs can new life arise. For Brewin, the primary way of understanding the importance of decay lies in understanding its necessity from an ecological point of view:

Without organic decomposers (bacteria and fungi) decaying dead organic matter, vital nutrients would be trapped and never be released back into the soil. Plants would therefore be unable to grow, and every ecosystem would collapse, as plants are at the base of every food chain: the cycle of life would grind to a halt. Not only that: if nothing decayed, the dead bodies of all living creatures and plants would litter the globe. We would literally be climbing over undecayed bodies.[1]

He goes on to note that there have been times in history when decay was largely absent. He notes that during the carboniferous period, "large quantities of wood were buried and not broken down because the bacteria and insects that could effectively digest them had not yet evolved."

For decay to happen, then, we need "agents of decay." These agents of decay are what enable the dead to break down and give way to new life. Without them, death remains the last word. Politically speaking, Brewin mentions the Occupy movement (an international protest against social and economic inequality) as an example of agents of decay in the political realm:

> Right-wing observers like to portray those involved [in the Occupy protests] as dirty maggots and bottom-feeders anyway, but this should perhaps be taken as a compliment. They are crawling over the dead matter, trying to work out what can yet be reused, and how these rich resources can fund new directions.[2]

In other words, the common critique that the Occupy movement does not provide a positive alternative obscures its deconstructive significance. The movement does not directly birth new forms of political life, but it helps to expose the decay of already dead forms.

Thus, the two roles that an agent of decay fulfills are confronting us with the death of the decaying thing in a visceral way and freeing up the raw materials necessary for new life.

The role of rituals within the radical collective is that of agents of decay that disintegrate the virtual power of the sacred-object so that new life arises. This enables us to follow Brewin in his reading of the verse that says, "Though outwardly we are decaying, yet inwardly we are being renewed day by day."[3] Instead of seeing it speaking negatively (about decay) then positively (about renewal), he sees the verse as making *two* positive claims that are directly connected.

The Disappearance of the Pastor

This enactment of decay in the structure of the liturgical space can be difficult, for it's tempting to try to create eternal structures that give ongoing security to those in leadership. Because of this, the effective church leader must be a true militant who holds the value of the process above any personal ambitions or fears, one who is willing to create structures that have "sell-by" dates and that might result in them being put out of a job.

The move that is made here is somewhat analogous to what we see in the old Canadian TV series *The Littlest Hobo*. The show centered on the life of a dog that traveled from place to place helping those in need. The dog had no owner, preferred to be alone, and would always leave quietly at the close of the episode. The narrative structure was generally the same: the show would begin with a situation of human conflict, and the mysterious dog would show up to help. As the episode progressed, the dog would function as a means of bringing reconciliation and reestablishing normality. Then, at the end, while everyone was celebrating, the dog would wander off down the road to find someone else to help.

The dog didn't seek to be the object of the community's love, but rather sought to create the conditions for a healthier community. In philosophical terms, the dog was a type of vanishing mediator that opened up the possibility of a transition between two states.

A subversive leader who wishes to be true to the event of Christianity is not concerned with getting people to buy into a particular set of beliefs or new tribal community. Rather, such a leader introduces people to a different way of life, one that not only breaks apart the strangle hold of dogmatic beliefs and destabilizes rigid community markers, but also one that makes the leader's ongoing presence ultimately superfluous. This means that the leader's final magic trick, after helping to reenact the Pledge, the Turn, and the Prestige of the sacred, must be to enact her own disappearance.

Just like with Jesus and his two disciples on the road to Emmaus, the show ends with the disappearance of the one who helped perform the trick.

CONCLUSION

In the Name

I'd like to close with a benediction by Pádraig Ó Tuama that gets to the heart of the event that I have struggled to reflect upon in the previous pages.

> In the name of goodness, of love and of broken
>   community
> In the name of meaning, of feeling and I hope you don't
>   screw me
> In the name of darkness, of light and ungraspable twilight
> In the name of mealtimes and sharing and caring by
>   firelight
>
> In the name of action, of peace and of human redemption
> In the name of eating of drinking, and table confession

In the name of sadness, regret and holy obsession
The holy name of anger, the spirit of aggression

In the name of Forgive and Forget, and I hope I get over this
In the name of father and son and the holy spirit
In the name of beauty and broken and beaten up daily
In the name of seeing our creeds and believing in maybe

We gather here . . . A table of strangers
And speak of our hopeland . . . And talk of our danger
To make sense of our thinking . . . To authenticate lives
To humanize feeling . . . And stop telling lies

In the name of Philosophy, of Theology and Who gives a
    damn
In the name of employment, and study and finding new
    family
In the name of our passions, our lovings and indecent
    obsessions
In the name of prayer, and of worship and demon
    possession

In the name of solitude, of quiet and holy reflection
the lost, the lonely and the without-direction
efficiency, stupidity, and the wholly ineffectual
the straight, and the queer, the transgender and bisexual

In the name of bootclogs, and boobjobs and erectile
    dysfunction,

schizophrenia, hysteria and obsessive compulsion
in the name of Jesus, and Mary and the mostly silent
    Joseph
in the name of speaking to ourselves saying "this is more
    than I can cope with."

In the name of touchup, and of breakup and of
    breakdown-and-weeping
therapy, and Prozac and of full-hearted breathing
sadness and madness and years-since-I've-smiled.
In the name of the Unknown, the Alien and of the
    Wholly-in-Exile.

In the name of goodness and kindness and intentionality
In the name of harbor, and shelter and family

Acknowledgments

⁕

A host of different elements must come together when writing a book, but amid all these two stand out for me. First, there is the spark that provokes me to write in the first place, and second, there is the fuel I use to feed the form my words take.

In typical fashion, the spark is testified to in the dedication of a work, while the fuel is found here, in the acknowledgments.

There are more influences behind this book than I could possibly name. Over the years many thinkers have been put on the often procrustean bed of my mind. Yet a few stand out, not only because of their insights, but because of the way that they have shaken me out of my orthodox slumbers and helped me look in unfamiliar ways at the familiar. This book in particular arises out of the philosophical and theological influences of Hegel, Jacques Lacan, Slavoj Žižek, and John D. Caputo. But added to this mix are the insights of Kester Brewin and the poetry of Pádraig Ó Tuama.

Then there are those who were invaluable in their support. There are Brian and Jill (to whom I am forever indebted), Josh (for his graphic skills and patience as I repeatedly changed

185

my mind over what the diagrams should look like), Andy (my eagle-eyed editor), Liz (who volunteered to work through the manuscript seeking out errors), and Philis (for her graciousness toward me as one deadline after another gently drifted by).

And then there are those who buy my books and wrestle with them, many of whom I've had the good fortune to meet as I travel and speak. There have been more times than I'd like to remember when I've questioned what I do. But then I stumble into some great conversation or find a deep connection with someone who first encountered me through the printed page, and it all makes a little more sense.

Notes

❧

INTRODUCTION

1. John Tillotson, *Sermons Preach'd Upon Several Occasions.* 1694 xxvi II 237.
2. 1 Corinthians 12:27.

CHAPTER 1

1. The diagrams in the book were directly inspired by those of Frederiek Depoortere in *Christ in Postmodern Philosophy* (London: T&T Clark, 2008).

CHAPTER 2

1. http://cavalorn.livejournal.com/584135.html.
2. Friedrich Nietzsche, *The Birth of Tragedy* (New York: Cambridge University Press, 1999).
3. www.psychologytoday.com/blog/all-about-addiction/201101/even-when-you-know-its-fake-the-strength-the-placebo-effect.

CHAPTER 3

1. Tacitus, Cornelius, *The Histories*, book 5, section 9; www.our civilisation.com/smartboard/shop/tacitusc/histries/chap18.htm.

CHAPTER 4

1. Romans 7:7–12.

CHAPTER 5

1. Søren Kierkegaard, *Fear and Trembling* (Radford: Wilder Publications, 2008), 29.
2. Ibid.
3. Slavoj Žižek, *Less Than Nothing* (London: Verso, 2012), 530.
4. 1 Corinthians 12:27.

CHAPTER 6

1. 1 Corinthians 1:22–25.
2. Hessert, Paul, *Christ and the End of Meaning* (London: Element Books, 1993), 20.
3. Ibid., 21.
4. Ibid.
5. Ibid., 23, emphasis his.
6. 1 Corinthians 13.
7. Colossians 2:8.

INTERLUDE

1. Luke 15:11–32.
2. Kester Brewin, *Mutiny* (London: Vaux, 2012).

3. Ibid., 118.
4. He also employs Peter Pan and the story of Odysseus to deepen his point.
5. Brewin, *Mutiny*, 126.
6. Ibid., 127.
7. Ibid., 129.
8. Ibid., 130.

CHAPTER 7

1. Acts 9:1–14.
2. Matthew 27:54.
3. Galatians 3:28.
4. 1 Corinthians 4:13.

CHAPTER 9

1. Brewin, *Mutiny*, 56.
2. www.kesterbrewin.com/2011/12/08/death_decay_rituals_2.
3. 2 Corinthians 4:16.

To keep up with Peter, visit peterrollins.net. There you will find out more about his work, his speaking engagements, and contact information. You will also find an archive of articles Peter has written and a sample of talks he's given around the world.

You can also keep track of his latest work on Twitter (@peterrollins) and Facebook (OrthodoxHeretic).

ALSO BY
PETER
ROLLINS

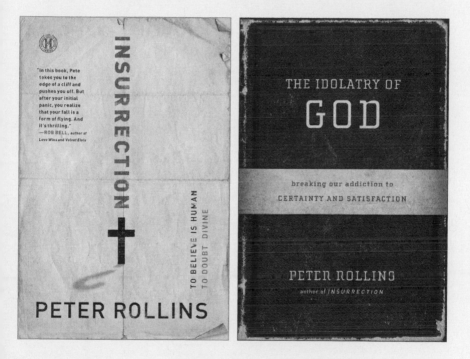

Available wherever books are sold
or at **SimonandSchuster.com**

Get email updates on

PETER ROLLINS,

exclusive offers,

and other great book recommendations

from Simon & Schuster.
